PRACTICAL SOCIAL WORK

Series Editor: Jo Campling

BASW

Editorial Advisory Board:
Robert Adams, Terry Bamford, Charles Barker,
Lena Dominelli, Malcolm Payne, Michael Preston-Shoot,
Daphne Statham and Jane Tunstill

Social work is at an important stage in its development. All professions must be responsive to changing social and economic conditions if they are to meet the needs of those they serve. This series focuses on sound practice and the specific contributions which social workers can make to the well-being of our society.

The British Association of Social Workers has always been conscious of its role in setting guidelines for practice and in seeking to raise professional standards. The conception of the Practical Social Work series arose from a survey of BASW members to discover where they, the practitioners in social work, felt there was the most need for new literature. The response was overwhelming and enthusiastic, and the result is a carefully planned, coherent series of books. The emphasis is firmly on practice set in a theoretical framework. The books will inform, stimulate and promote discussion, thus adding to the further development of skills and high professional standards. All the authors are practitioners and teachers of social work representing a wide variety of experience.

JO CAMPLING

A list of published titles in this series follows overleaf

PRACTICAL SOCIAL WORK

Dealing with Stress

Neil Thompson
Michael Murphy
and
Steve Stradling

MACMILLAN

First published 1994 by
THE MACMILLAN PRESS LTD
Houndmills, Basingstoke, Hampshire RG21 2XS
and London
Companies and representatives
throughout the world

ISBN 0–333–60004–5 hardcover
ISBN 0–333–60005–3 paperback

A catalogue record for this book
is available from the British Library.

Copy-edited and typeset by Povey–Edmondson
Okehampton and Rochdale, England

Printed in Hong Kong

Series Standing Order (Practical Social Work)

If you would like to receive future titles in this series as they are
published, you can make use of our standing order facility. To
place a standing order please contact your bookseller or, in case
of difficulty, write to us at the address below with your name and
address and the name of the series. Please state with which title
you wish to begin your standing order. (If you live outside the
UK we may not have the rights for your area, in which case we
will forward your order to the publisher concerned.)

Standing Order Service, Macmillan Distribution Ltd,
Houndmills, Basingstoke, Hampshire, RG21 2XS, England.

Contents

List of Figures

Preface

Social work is widely recognised as an occupation strongly associated with pressure and stress. Dealing with the pain, distress and suffering brought about by crisis, loss, abuse, poverty, social problems and oppression, is bound to leave its mark on the worker. No one coming into social work with their eyes open can fail to see the difficulties and challenges inherent in this type of work. In addition to these inherent factors, we must also recognise, and take account of, a range of other pressures which, whilst not inevitable, are very much part of the modern social work scene. These include resource constraints, frequent and rapid change, unhelpful management practices and a disregard for the importance of supporting staff through the sometimes immense demands and complexities of their work.

This book has been written not as a guaranteed antidote to stress, but rather as a text that can offer guidance on how we can equip ourselves to deal as effectively as possible with the stresses we face in modern social work. The book is offered in a spirit of cautious optimism. We fully acknowledge the vast range of pressures practitioners and managers are required to cope with and how destructive these pressures can prove to be – for clients, workers and social work as a whole. However, counterbalanced against this, we also acknowledge the huge value of adopting a positive and assertive approach towards these pressures. This book is premised on our firm belief that there is much that can be done to maintain those pressures within manageable limits, to create a supportive and constructive atmosphere and to generate much needed feelings of job satisfaction and professional worth. We do not promise that this comes easy but we do believe that a defeatist attitude of pessimism is a barrier to positive outcomes for service users and a healthy and fulfilling work environment for service providers.

The guidance we offer here is based on the research, training and consultancy work undertaken by the Stress in Social Work Research Group since 1990. The book is a collaborative effort by three members of the group. Neil Thompson, a social work tutor with many years' experience of practice and management, has been the main author and co-ordinator of the project. Michael Murphy, an experienced child care practitioner and child protection training officer, has also made a significant contribution, including the majority of the 'Practice Focus' illustrations used at various points in the text. Steve Stradling is a Senior Lecturer in Psychology at the University of Manchester and has acted as the 'anchor' for the project, providing advice and support relating to issues of statistical analysis and research methodology.

Stress is a major issue in social work and one which deserves far more detailed study and attention than it currently receives. We hope that this book can offer social work staff – both practitioners and managers – some informed guidance on how to deal with stress and related issues and, in the process, play at least a small part in achieving a higher profile for issues of stress and staff care.

NEIL THOMPSON

Acknowledgements

This book has been written by three members of the Stress in Social Work Research Group but credit must also be given to a fourth member of the group, Paul O'Neill, first, for his involvement in the research work which informs this book and, second, for the use of ideas and material drawn from his MSc dissertation on 'Stress in Social Work'.

We are grateful to Margaret Hodgkinson for doing such a good job of typing the manuscripts and, in addition, to Anne Paterson for her sterling administrative support throughout the project. We should also acknowledge our debt to the hundreds of social work staff who played a part in the development of this book by contributing to the research study to which we refer at various points in the text. We hope that they and their colleagues will benefit from the results.

NEIL THOMPSON

The author and publishers are grateful to McGraw-Hill Book Co, for permission to reproduce Figure 1.1, taken from Arroba and James (1987) *Pressure at Work: A Survival Guide*, and to Tony Morrison for permission to use Figure 7.1, which is based on his training materials.

Introduction

There are many books available which give advice and guidance on stress management techniques and how to 'look after yourself'. This, however, is not simply another book about coping with the effects of work and life pressures. This text is different in a number of ways:

1. Traditional approaches to stress adopt a narrow and individualistic perspective with little attention paid to the wider organisational, social and political factors involved. This text locates issues of stress firmly within the context of the way social work organisations function and the conflicting expectations society has of social workers.
2. This book is specifically related to social work concerns and addresses issues which relate directly to the management and practice of social work. Actual social work examples are used to illustrate many of the points raised.
3. Although this is primarily a practical book, it is not simply a prescriptive guide based just on 'common sense' or the personal experience of the authors. It is based on a clearly articulated theoretical framework of the complexities and intricacies of the workings of stress in social work. It is also based on empirical research carried out in three English local authority Social Services Departments (see below). The findings of this research project are used, along with a wide range of other research studies, to illustrate and support points covered in the text. In short, this is a practical book, but one grounded in theory and research.

Throughout this text we introduce findings from a study we conducted in 1990. Responses to an extensive questionnaire were obtained from 283 field social workers in three local authority Social Services Departments in the north-west of England, and 49 residential social work staff in one of these authorities. As well as providing basic demographic details and information about their social work experience, the respondents completed a brief measure of anxiety and depression, rated the stressfulness of a range of social work tasks and features, indicated their preferred coping styles, the level and type of support they received from fellow workers, and the levels of satisfaction they obtained from various aspects of their role as social workers. (Further details of this study may be obtained from the authors.)

The book's title, *Dealing with Stress*, is particularly significant in so far as it is deliberately ambiguous. It refers to three separate processes:

- preventing the pressures we face from becoming harmful and destructive; that is, *avoiding* stress
- minimising and counteracting the harmful effects of stress when our attempts at prevention have broken down; that is, *coping with* stress
- readjusting after a prolonged or heavy period of stress or a particularly traumatic and stressful event; that is, *recovering from* stress

Social work as an occupation is characterised by a wide range of pressures and dilemmas, involving emotional demands, potential conflicts and threats or even actual violence. In addition, there is frequent exposure to the pain, suffering and distress of others, the full weight of the human condition. All this needs to be seen in the context of resource constraints, legal requirements, organisational pressures and media attention. Given this scenario, it is not surprising that social work and social care are often experienced as stressful.

A major aim of this book, therefore, is to cast light on the potential sources of stress for social work staff and the development of appropriate strategies (at both the level of the individual and the organisation) for coping with stress and for preventing stress in the first place.

The book is divided into eight chapters. Chapter 1 focuses on the costs of stress and thereby emphasises why it is important to devote our attention to these issues. Chapter 2 outlines a theory base which will act as a foundation for our approach to dealing with stress. A three-dimensional model of stress is presented and the applicability of this to social work is considered. The main focus, in this chapter, is on 'stressors', the sources of pressure which can give rise to stress. This chapter outlines the theoretical distinction between pressure, which can be positive or negative, depending on the context in which it is experienced, and stress, which is always harmful and destructive. We seek to enable social work staff to distinguish between the two and thus be in a position to use pressure constructively and positively but without allowing it to 'overspill' and become stress.

Chapter 3 addresses the personal, psychological aspects of stress and stress-management. In particular, it considers the variety of coping methods available to us. Chapter 4 builds on this by exploring some of the wider social issues – in particular, race and gender – that influence the experience of stress in social work. This chapter relates stress to issues of equality of opportunity and anti-discriminatory practice. It shows how traditional approaches to stress which focus on the individual run the risk of neglecting vitally important aspects of the situation such as the oppressive effects of racism and sexism.

Chapters 5 and 6 discuss the wider context of stress in social work. They develop a discussion of the potentially stressful factors which are intrinsic to social work; that is, those which are an inherent part of the social work task, for example, the care versus control dilemma. Chapter 5 considers ways in which these stressors can be minimised and how our attitude towards them is a significant factor in determining whether or not they are experienced as stressful.

Chapter 6 follows a similar path, but concentrates instead on those pressures which are extrinsic to social work; that is, factors which can, in theory at least, be avoided or eliminated, for example, a lack of supervision or training. The focus here is on the organisational context of social work, and is therefore of particular relevance to managers and policy makers, as well as basic grade practitioners.

Chapter 7 focuses on the steps that can be taken to:

- prevent pressure overspilling into stress
- cope with stress when it does arise
- deal with the aftermath of particularly stressful or traumatic incidents or periods

It concentrates on adopting a pragmatic and effective way of dealing with stress issues. In particular, it argues the case for organisations developing clear and realistic staff care policies.

Chapter 8 is the concluding chapter. It attempts to draw together the main strands of the arguments and summarises our approach to dealing with stress. It seeks to bring together the diverse themes which recur throughout the book in order to leave the reader with an overall view of dealing with stress in social work – an overview which will, we hope, help to equip staff to deal as effectively as possible with the multitude of pressures they face.

The book has been written with a wide audience in mind. We hope it will be of direct relevance to practitioners in all aspects of social work – field, residential, day care and so on. We also feel this is a book for managers, partly in terms of managing their own pressures and stresses, but also in terms of fulfilling their duty of supporting their staff in coping with the particular pressures they encounter in their practice. In a sense, then, this book is doubly important for managers and supervisors.

This book will not provide you with everything you need to deal with the stresses of modern social work – no book can do that. What it will do, we very much hope, is give you a knowledge base, a theoretical framework for extending that knowledge base and some of the skills and strategies you need to give of your best without doing harm to your own health or well-being. In particular, we hope it will give you – individually and collectively – the confidence and determination to succeed in this task.

1

The Costs of Stress

What is stress?

The term 'stress' is used in everyday speech in a loose and non-specific way to refer broadly to the process of coping with life's pressures and problems and the negative feelings this can generate. However, in order to study stress and its effects, causes and so on, we need a more precise definition – a degree of academic rigour is called for.

The *Concise Oxford Dictionary* defines stress as a 'demand on energy'. The way the term is used in occupational psychology extends the concept somewhat, as illustrated by the following quotation from Torrington *et al.* (1985): 'Stress is a demand made on our physical or mental energy. Where this is felt as excessive, it is experienced as stressful and may lead to stress-related physiological problems' (p. 39).

However, even this extension of the term is not sufficient for our purposes, in three ways:

1. It is too narrow: It refers to the physiological effects of stress but not the psychological, social, organisational or financial implications.
2. It is also too broad: The word 'stress' refers to both the actual pressures we face and the effects of these pressures. That is, 'stress' refers to both 'pressure' (contributory/causal factor) and 'strain' (the costs of such pressure).
3. It is misleading: It implies that stress is only harmful when pressure is excessive. It ignores the stress which can be brought about by insufficient pressure or understimulation.

1

We therefore need to take matters a step further in order to overcome these weaknesses. As far as 1. is concerned we need to adopt a more holistic perspective on stress so that it is fully realised that stress is not simply a medical or psychological entity; it operates at a variety of levels. We need to recognise stress as a multifaceted phenomenon.

As for 2., a useful terminological distinction here is that between stress and pressure. Pressure is something we all face as life makes its various demands upon us. It is not necessarily problematical and is, in fact, very often a significant source of energy, motivation and pleasure. However, when the level of pressure becomes harmful, counterproductive or in any way negative, the term 'stress' then becomes applicable. That is, pressure is neutral – it can be positive or negative – whereas stress is always negative, it is where the pressure starts to do harm. (Spielberger, 1979, amongst others, uses a parallel distinction but refers to stress versus strain in place of our pressure versus stress.)

Arroba and James (1987) capture the distinction well when they comment that:

> Pressure and stress are words which are often used inter-changeably. They are not in fact the same. Everyone needs a certain amount of pressure. Pressure can lead to stress. No one needs stress . . . Stress is your response to an inappropriate level of pressure. It is a response to pressure, not the pressure itself (p. 3).

This passage also relates to point 3. above. The key phrase is 'inappropriate level of pressure'. This is not simply too much pressure, but can also refer to too little pressure. If our lives are not sufficiently interesting or stimulating – if not enough demands are made upon us – this in itself becomes stressful. As Arroba and James put it: 'Both high pressure and low pressure are inappropriate and thus stressful' (p. 3). In fact, they provide a helpful diagram which portrays this vividly and succinctly (Figure 1.1: the arrow represents the continuum of pressure, from high at the top to low at the bottom).

Figure 1.1 *The stress continuum*

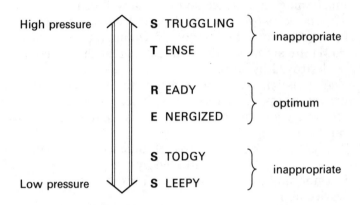

High pressure	**S** TRUGGLING
	T ENSE } inappropriate
	R EADY
	E NERGIZED } optimum
	S TODGY
Low pressure	**S** LEEPY } inappropriate

Source: Arroba and James (1987).

This conception of stress is of particular significance as it will be a central theme of our argument that social work managers have a responsibility to ensure that, as far as possible, their staff operate within the optimal middle range.

Within this text the term 'stress' will therefore be used, in line with Arroba and James, to refer to the negative subjective response to an inappropriate level of pressure. This, in itself, has major implications for how we deal with stress as it indicates that the impact of stress hinges on both the objective dimension – the level of pressure – and the subjective dimension of the individual's response to such pressure.

Paying the price for stress

One of the main reasons why stress is such an important area of study is its heavy cost in terms of the damage it does to individuals, to relationships and to organisations. The costs of stress can therefore be seen to operate at four separate but interconnected levels. These are:

1. *The personal or psychological.* This includes the possible detrimental effects on health, mental and emotional functioning, confidence and general well-being.
2. *The social and interpersonal.* Interpersonal relationships, teamwork, contribution to the community and earning power are amongst the social factors that can be damaged or destroyed by stress.
3. *The organisational.* Stress tends to be very costly to organisations in terms of reduced productivity and efficiency, low morale, high sickness and staff turnover rates and so on.
4. *The professional.* Standards of practice and quality of service can be adversely affected by stress. In the long run, it is not only staff who suffer as a result of stress but also service users.

It is worth exploring each of these in a little more detail in order to develop a clearer picture of the impact of stress in its various manifestations and, in so doing, lay the foundations for the later discussions on the subject of tackling the stress-related problems social work staff so frequently encounter.

The personal costs

One of the most significant, and most worrying, effects of stress is its detrimental impact on health. Most, if not all, medical conditions can be seen to be exacerbated by stress and many, it is argued, are actually largely caused by stress (Coleman, 1988). Similarly, the effects of stress on mental health are also not inconsiderable. Indeed, it is useful to consider the personal costs of stress in terms of the three aspects of health: stress-related illness, exacerbation of other medical conditions and the impact on mental health.
    Stress-related illnesses include:

• ulcerative colitis
• heart disease
• high blood pressure
• asthma
• migraine

We are not saying that stress is the sole *cause* of these conditions but, rather, that there is a very close and strong relationship between stress and medical problems such as these.

We can also see that stress has a more general effect on health. Totman (1990) relates this specifically to the links between stress and the immune system:

> We now know that the immune system is involved in the control of health in a very wide range of conditions, including cancer. We also know that there is an intimate system of communication between the brain and the immune system, and that the immune system is easily upset by hormones released in times of stress. There is now clear evidence that psychological states like depression, stress and the failure to cope with problems disable the immune system in various ways and interfere with its health-protecting function (p. 15).

Prolonged exposure to stress can have a very damaging impact on health (Melhuish, 1978) through its detrimental effects on the body's biochemistry, for example, by an increased production of stomach acid leading to ulcers of the stomach or duodenum. Quick and Quick (1984) also note that stress has been identified as a contributory factor in a wide range of health problems, such as headaches, backache and skin diseases. Indeed, it is widely recognised that stress issues are likely to exacerbate health problems and hamper recovery.

As far as mental health is concerned, there are also close links with stress. In particular, stress has been associated with anxiety and depression. The link between stress and anxiety is control. Both stress and anxiety are characterised by a perceived lack of personal control over one's life. Between stress and depression is the common theme of loss of meaning, purpose or direction and perhaps also loss of control.

In fact, we can even go so far as to criticise orthodox psychiatry for its underestimation of the role of stress in mental disorder. As Heather (1976) argues:

Psychiatrists have recently become excited by the surprising, to them, discovery that 'life-events', such as bereavements, marriages, and changes of job, often precede the onset of psychiatric illness. Even here, though, the relation between the event and the illness is presented in a compartmentalized, mechanical fashion; little or no attempt is made to integrate both life-events and 'illness' in a biographically significant account of the person's experience of life (p. 79).

Heather's point is that a medical model of mental health problems readily leads us into a perspective which, in its desire to achieve scientific respectability, pays inadequate attention to the life pressures that people face and the influence of these pressures on mental well-being.

Overall, the effects of stress and burnout (a related concept we shall discuss below) upon our physical and mental health can indeed be seen to constitute a major cause for concern. Many people experience ill-health – at varying levels of severity – partly, or even largely, as a result of exposure to high levels of stress; in some cases it even proves fatal.

In addition to the health-related costs of stress, there are, of course, other personal costs, including a negative impact on:

- confidence and self esteem
- job satisfaction and opportunities for professional development
- the ability to keep things in proportion and form balanced judgements.
- fulfilling personal potential and making effective use of time
- the ability to relax and enjoy life

Furthermore, the other types of cost that we shall discuss below, for example, the social costs, also have repercussions at a personal level – just as many of the personal costs outlined here have wider implications for others and for organisations.

The social and interpersonal costs

Stress has implications not only for the individual but also with regard to interpersonal relations and other social factors.

The social and interpersonal costs are recognised as particularly detrimental as they can be seen to be 'contagious',
metaphorically speaking; that is, stress experienced by one
group of workers can 'infect' other groups of staff. For
example, if a social work team is under a great deal of pressure
the effects of this can 'rub off' on other staff such as admin.
workers or other colleagues.

Practice Focus 1.1

Alison was a new unit manager. At first the team
believed that her rushed and anxious demeanour was
merely due to the adjustment to her new role. But, as the
months rolled by, the team began to realise that she was
a 'stress carrier', someone who could increase their
anxiety and pressure levels just by being there. Wherever
she went people would feel stressed and often seek a
convenient excuse to leave the room.

One particularly significant way in which this manifests
itself is through strain on relationships, both personal and
professional. Irritability, impatience and a short temper
frequently accompany stress, and so it is not surprising that
stress can be very detrimental to relationships. It is not
uncommon for people under stress to become quite
unapproachable, and this makes it difficult for others to
offer support, or for such offers of support to be accepted.
Severe stress can produce a 'suffering skin' in which a
protective psychological layer develops in order to protect
the person concerned from the stressors. The main problem
with this, however, is that it also shields out the positive
aspects of the job, as well as personal coping and staff care
support.

Strained relationships can also be accompanied by tension,
anxiety or even depression. These factors can be both the

cause and the result of strained relationships. In fact, it is not unusual for a vicious circle to develop in which the two sets of issues reinforce each other and thus contribute to an even higher level of stress. In this sense we can say that 'stress begets stress'. This is one of the many ways in which stress can be seen to be cyclical (Thompson, 1991a).

Stress can also magnify or accentuate aspects of people's personalities or their characteristic ways of relating to other people. For example, someone who has a slight tendency towards aggression at times may become markedly more aggressive as a result of excessive pressure – this may be his or her 'response to an inappropriate level of pressure'. Similarly, a slightly shy person may become very withdrawn and uncommunicative. Both types of behaviour have their costs in terms of teamwork and collaboration, especially in relation to multidisciplinary work where the potential for tension and conflict is much higher, as is the need for effective communication.

Stress can therefore place a considerable strain on teams or other work groups. This is very much the case when a significant number of team members are experiencing stress at the same time (that is, not just pressure, but enough pressure to be causing harm). Whole teams can and do experience stress for a variety of reasons – shortage of staff, policy changes or management decisions, reorganisation or a threat to the team's continued existence and so on – and this can make the team a very unhealthy environment to be working in. Instead of being a significant source of support, the team can become a major additional source of pressure. As Morrison *et al.* (1987) put it:

> Teams need to be viable to achieve the tasks for which they were established. In practice often the'team' is not viable, but individuals within it are carrying out the agency objectives. What this means is that the additional support, creativity, and energy which a healthy team can give is not being used, and, more worryingly in some teams, energy for the task is actually being diverted into surviving or coping with the Team (p. 22).

The organisational costs

Workers in a poor state of physical and mental health are more likely to be inefficient and possibly more of a liability than an asset. As we have seen, poor or strained working relationships will also have their impact. But, moreover, the combination of these two sets of factors can spell major problems for an organisation. We would therefore argue that it is important for organisations to ensure that workers do not experience any unnecessary stress, and that they feel in a position to take action should they be under intolerable levels of pressure. Indeed, this is the basis of staff care and one of the fundamental principles of human resource management.

Various studies have shown that for those in employment, occupation tends to be the major source of stress (Warr and Payne, 1982; Newton and Keenan, 1985). In certain occupations such as the caring professions, including social work of course, stress can be seen to be especially prevalent; in fact, it is virtually seen as endemic – an occupational hazard.

Fineman (1985) found in his research on stress amongst social workers that experiencing high levels of pressure was perceived as part of the job, part of the organisational culture. Within such helping professions, however, the effects of stress are more marked, with higher levels of burnout, and mental health problems being reported.

Stress is known to affect job satisfaction, performance and productivity. Lower levels of performance and productivity mean that the organisation is achieving less than it could if stress levels were lower. This also renders the services provided more expensive than they need to be, thereby giving less value for money for the general public who foot the bill. As we shall emphasise below, in the caring professions high levels of pressure and stressed workers can mean poor service delivery – or even a dangerous style of practice as, for example, in child protection work (Dale *et al.*, 1986).

In addition, absenteeism is a major cost to the employer, and indications are that in many occupations it is becoming a growing problem. Cooper *et al.* (1988) note that, by the 1970s it was recognised that time lost from stress-related illnesses cost Britain far more time than was lost due to work stoppages. Kearns (1986) estimated that 60 per cent of absences from work are caused by stress-related illness and that in the UK over 100 million days were lost due to the fact that people could not face going to work. And the effect of absenteeism is, of course, a cumulative one as the absence of colleagues places greater work pressures on those who do turn up for work (see Figure 1.2).

Various researchers have found that stress can also lead to a high staff turnover rate – another high cost that employing organisations have to bear (Jones *et al.*, 1991; Arnold and Feldman, 1982). Whilst the actual cost of employee turnover is difficult to calculate, and it will differ according to occupation, Quick and Quick (1984) estimate that, on average, the cost is often equal to five times the employee's monthly salary.

In 1991 the number of applicants for social work training places in the United Kingdom was down by 1000. One of the main reasons given for the decline is the high stress levels (as reported in *Community Care*, 31 January 1991). As with absenteeism, this can easily become a vicious circle in which recruitment difficulties and high staff turnover combine to produce staff shortages. Such shortages, in turn, produce a greater workload and thus extra pressure for the staff that remain. The ensuing high levels of stress combine with a low level of morale which further increases the problems of recruitment and retention. And so it goes on.

The professional costs

Poor standards of work in a social work context can, of course, have disastrous consequences. For example, McGee (1989) in a study of child protection workers, found a link between burnout and decision making. Those workers who deny the need for involvement, a dominant feature amongst those who are suffering from burnout, tend to utilise 'defence-avoidance' behaviour in order to ward off anxiety. This may lead to a failure to address important aspects of the case and thus contribute to poor decision making. And, as we have indicated, in child protection work – as in many other aspects of social work – poor decisions can be extremely dangerous

Figure 1.2 *Recruitment and retention problems*

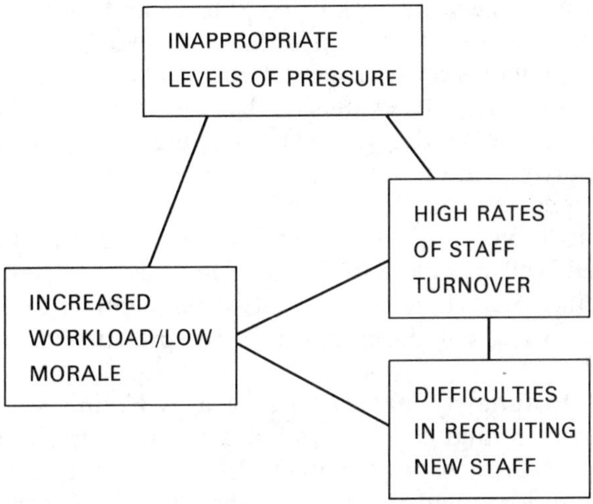

decisions for client and worker alike. If we examine many child care inquiries closely, we can speculate with hindsight that such defence-avoidance behaviour contributed to the poor practice which played a part in the death or serious injury of a child (DOH, 1991a).

Perhaps the most significant social cost of stress is bad or dangerous professional practice. This can come about through poor communication, poor concentration or attention to detail, a lack of commitment or, perhaps most worrying of all, an inability/unwillingness to listen, or respond, to other people's pain.

Practice Focus 1.2

Colin had worked for many years as a residential worker before switching over to fieldwork. He found it difficult to adjust to working on his own most of the time and missed the strong sense of teamwork and shared responsibility he had previously enjoyed. He found his new role very stressful, as was clearly shown by his high level of anxiety, his lack of confidence and the generally chaotic nature of his approach to the work. The stress was having a very detrimental effect on the standards of his work as was evidenced by the large number of mistakes he made. His new colleagues wanted to be supportive but felt it was only a matter of time before he returned to residential work where he felt more comfortable and in control. Indeed, despite having coped well in one very demanding area of social work practice, he found himself out of his depth in what, in many ways, could be seen as a less pressurised area of work.

Unfortunately, his team leader took Colin's strengths for granted and had therefore not deemed it necessary to support him through a difficult period of adjustment. Despite his obvious strengths, the stress he experienced in fieldwork resulted in poor practice and an unsatisfactory level of service for the people he worked with.

Burnard (1991) discusses the tendency for stressed workers in the caring professions to treat service users as objects, to deny them their humanity:

We can probably all recall times when, under stress, we have treated patients or clients as objects. Sometimes we label the 'It' an 'appendectomy' or a 'case'. While, if we can allow ourselves a moment's thought, we know that underneath this label there are other persons with thoughts, feelings, families and all sorts of problems, and yet we can find no other way of coping with them at this particular moment other than by seeing them as clinical objects (p. 34).

Stress therefore acts as a barrier to effective and rewarding practice which, in turn, has several potential or actual costs, including:

- poor quality of service
- lack of job satisfaction
- a negative, cynical and demoralised atmosphere
- a lack of public faith in social work

Quick and Quick (1984) note that stress can cause a number of indirect costs. These include loss of vitality, as well as the communication breakdown and faulty decision making referred to above. Loss of vitality may lead to low morale, low motivation and high dissatisfaction. Ultimately this will lead to burnout and to poor provision of services. Burnout is a condition closely linked to stress and is characterised by three distinct but related phenomena (see Maslach and Jackson, 1981):

- emotional exhaustion
- lack of individual achievement
- depersonalisation (see the quotation from Burnard, 1991, above)

The overall effect of burnout is a very destructive one, leaving the staff concerned feeling bitter, disillusioned and demotivated – and therefore unlikely to achieve high standards of professional practice. They become locked into a cycle of negativism in which their morale and well-being suffer, as do the effectiveness of the organisation, the interests of service users and the profession of social work as a whole.

Conclusion

As we have seen, the effects of stress are not restricted to individuals but may also spread to have a serious impact on other social groups including colleagues and clients. Organisations, like individuals, have their own idiosyncratic needs and stressors which first have to be identified before any meaningful long-lasting work can be carried out aimed at reducing the effects of stress. There can be no single formula solution to an organisation's ills but there are, of course, commonalities which can be recognised. Some of these common issues and patterns will be considered in Chapter 6.

The costs of stress for organisations are many and varied and there is a considerable body of literature which explores the various aspects. Space does not permit a more detailed analysis of the organisational and financial costs of stress but this brief overview shows that stress is an important and costly issue not just for staff within an organisation but also for the organisation itself in terms of how efficiently and effectively it operates and how healthy an environment it provides for its staff and service users. For social work organisations this is a particularly important observation as social work is, of course, characterised by pressure, tension, conflict and contradictions, as the discussions in Chapter 5 will emphasise.

Having considered, in outline at least, the various costs of stress, we can now move on to examine other aspects of pressure and stress in order to develop a strategy – or set of strategies – for keeping such costs to a minimum. We shall begin by exploring the various sources of stress and relating these to the theoretical framework which underpins the remainder of the book.

2

Sources of Stress

In order to develop an understanding of sources of stress, it is necessary to locate the issues of stress and pressure within a theoretical context – to appreciate the subtle and complex factors which lead to certain aspects of personal or work experience being, in some way, distressing or detrimental to one's well-being. It is therefore necessary to preface a discussion of social work stressors with a brief outline of a theoretical model which helps cast light on the factors and processes which contribute to social work being experienced as stressful.

This chapter begins, then, with an exposition of the main points of the theoretical model on which the discussions in this book are based; that is, it sets the scene for understanding the concepts and issues explored in the remainder of the book by clarifying the conceptual framework which underpins our analysis of stress in social work.

The theory base

The theory base we are using is a 'three-dimensional' one (see Figure 2.1) which consists of the following three elements:

1. Stressors – the situational factors that contribute to the experience of stress.
2. Coping methods – the skills and strategies we develop as a means of coping with life's stresses and pressures.
3. Support systems – the range of supports, both formal and informal, which can be drawn upon.

Figure 2.1   *The three dimensions of stress*

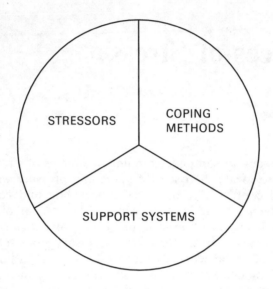

Most texts on the subject of stress tend to focus on 1 and 2. but have little or nothing to say on the subject of 3. For example, Looker and Gregson (1989) regard support simply as one coping method amongst others. When viewed from a management perspective, the relative neglect of this dimension is particularly significant. It is also of particular significance when stress in social work is the topic under scrutiny, for social work is characterised by attempts to support other people under stress and in distress. In this book, care is therefore taken not to neglect the issues of support.

Stress and social work

In many ways, stress can be seen as a central part of social work in so far as much of social work practice consists of intervening in situations where clients are under stress (that is, subject to inappropriate levels of pressure). Whether it be counselling or social care planning (Barclay Committee,

1982), the social work task is rarely, if ever, unconnected with stress. Indeed, the situations social workers face are often characterised by a debilitating level or intensity of stress.

The discussions about stress in the sections that follow will therefore cast at least some light on actual social work practice with clients. However, this is not the primary aim as our focus is to be on stress as experienced by social workers, and thus the implications for social work staff themselves – and, of course, their managers.

Just how stressful social work is remains a matter for debate and investigation. (A number of studies have been published on this topic – Gibson *et al.*, 1989; NALGO, 1989; Jones *et al.*, 1991). However, what is worth commenting on at this stage is a concept often closely associated with social work, that of 'burnout'. This denotes a stage which some people reach where prolonged stress has produced a state of apathy and disillusionment. The phenomenon of burnout is not restricted to social work yet seems to manifest itself more frequently in the 'caring professions' than in comparable high pressure occupations, as Edelwich and Brodsky confirm:

> The physical symptoms of Burnout that are commonly observed in human services personnel – ulcers, backaches, headaches, frequent colds, sexual problems – can just as easily be found in the high pressure world of business. And yet, Burnout does not occur with anything like the same regularity or carry with it the same social costs as it does in the human services, where it takes on a special character and a special intensity (1980, p. 15).

The same authors identify eight contributory factors which they use to try to explain why this should be so. These include low pay, inadequate institutional support and popular misunderstanding and suspicion. This last point is particularly relevant for child protection workers, given the high media profile of such work. The existence and impact of burnout needs to be acknowledged as it is clearly something both practitioners and managers would wish to eradicate.

Social workers are each day dealing with other people's stress and distress: they often face hostility, conflicting

Practice Focus 2.1

Aled had worked in the same team for eleven years since first qualifying as a social worker. In the early stages of his career, he had been very outspoken and less than tactful in his criticism of the area management team's running of the office. Consequently, he had become quite unpopular and had seriously limited his chances of career progression. Before too long he became 'stale' and lost his initial enthusiasm and commitment. This continued for a number of years without causing any major problems. However, at a time when the team faced a number of changes, Aled's attitude became even more negative and cynical to the point where his friends and colleagues began to lose patience with him. He became increasingly apathetic towards his clients and his workload in general. First of all, one client made a complaint about his brusque attitude and his tendency not to listen. Two weeks later, a further two clients exercised their rights under the Department's new Complaints and Representations procedure. It was at this point that Aled went on sick leave with 'nervous exhaustion' and his colleagues wondered whether he would ever return.

demands and expectations and, these days especially, they operate in a political climate which is inhospitable to social work and its values. Given this scenario, it therefore comes as no great surprise that the argument here should be for an understanding of dealing with stress to be high on the agenda for social work managers, educators and practitioners.

Some social work agencies have already recognised this. For example, Cheshire County Council, amongst others, have explicitly declared that they see their staff as their most valuable resource (see LGTB, 1988). However, how this can become more than rhetoric and actually realised in concrete terms remains to be clarified. What we now need to do, in order to further this aim, is to explore the causes and contributory factors, that is the 'stressors'.

Stressors

As mentioned above, the theoretical model presented here is a three-factor one, involving stressors, coping methods and support systems. All three aspects can be seen as 'causes' or 'contributory factors' but in this section we shall concentrate on stressors, the ideas, events, entities or processes which 'up the stakes' in terms of the pressures and demands which each day confront us. We shall examine a number of such stressors and comment briefly on their significance within a social work context.

Role stress is the first such stressor to be considered. There are several forms of role stress, as the following examples illustrate:

1. *Role ambiguity.* This arises when there is uncertainty about the scope of our responsibility, the expectations of others, how our work is to be evaluated and so on.
2. *Role incompatibility.* This refers to conflicting expectations, for example, those of clients versus those of management.
3. *Role conflict.* This arises when we receive conflicting messages concerning what is expected of us. The conflict can be due to conflicting messages coming from different persons (inter-sender role conflict) or the discrepancy in messages can actually arise from the same source (intra-sender role conflict – Khan *et al.*, 1964).
4. *Role overload.* This occurs when someone is expected to play too many roles.

Role stress is characterised by tension, low morale and communication difficulties (see Handy, 1985). This is a good example of how stress is not simply a matter of individual pathology (that is, a low tolerance of pressure) but also has a strong organisational dimension, in so far as the role structure of an organisation can play a major part.

Role stress can be seen as very much part and parcel of social work. All four examples cited above can no doubt easily be recognised within the social work world. Social work roles are often unclear, manifold and contradictory as indeed are the problems and issues social workers tackle. Preston-Shoot and Braye (1991) follow a similar line of argument in their discussion of role uncertainty:

> Social work contains practice dilemmas which emanate from contradictory public and political expectations. They arise from an absence of consensus on key questions which daily confront practitioners and their managers: when protection of vulnerable people (risk factors) must assume paramountcy over rights (self-determination); when an ethical duty of care must be expressed in the form of statutory control; what is good-enough child care; how agencies should intervene to protect older people from abuse or (self-)neglect (p. 17).

Smith *et al.* (1982) present six main causes of stress as follows:

(a) *Work*. Work can be stressful when there is too much of it, too little or, indeed, if it is too difficult. Clearly, in social work, too much work is a fact of life due to the infinite demand measured against finite supply. Similarly, the work is often extremely difficult, for example, receiving a child into care or dealing with a bereavement.

(b) *Uncertainty*. This overlaps with role stress above. Uncertainty and conflicting demands raise anxiety levels and thus fuel stress. This is particularly applicable to social work which is characterised by uncertainty and conflict (see Thompson, 1990).

(c) *Relations at work*. Poor working relationships can considerably raise pressure levels and thus prove stressful. This is particularly the case, argue Smith *et al.* (1982), when there is mistrust between employees. Mistrust is not generally associated with relationships between social work colleagues, but as value issues are predominant in social work, conflictual relations are not uncommon. For example, in our study of three local authorities, only 59 per cent of social workers agreed with the statement: 'The majority of my colleagues have similar values to mine.' Similarly, pressure can arise as a result of race and gender conflicts, for example in relation to issues of harassment.

(d) *Career prospects*. The problem here can manifest itself in two ways – overpromotion or underpromotion. The former relates to a situation in which an employee is promoted to a position which goes beyond his or her level of competence (the 'Peter Principle'). The latter refers to the frustration that arises as a result of unrealised or disappointed ambitions. Both these scenarios can be seen to apply to social work. Many excellent practitioners become managers only to find that their practice skills do not stand them in good stead. Equally, there are significant numbers of experienced workers who seek a new challenge but do not have the opportunity.

(e) *Organisational climate*. This may act as an inhibitor of an individual's freedom and creativity. A stifling organisa- tion may limit our personal control and thus cause frustration and resentment. Equally, an organisation which lacks control can generate feelings of insecurity and fear. Social work agencies vary considerably in terms of how controlling they are or of how overcontrolling they may be and many find it difficult to remain within the constructive centre of the range by avoiding the two extremes of being overcontrolling and being dangerously uncontrolled.

(f) *Balance between work and home life*. There can easily arise a conflict or imbalance between the two areas. In social work this may be when too many evening visits disrupt home life or when home pressures overspill into work patterns.

The two classifications so far considered are both predominantly work-focused and pay little attention to wider sources of stress. One approach which does not fall into this trap is that of Holmes and Rahe (1967) who provide a 'league table' of stress-inducing life events, ranging from the death of a spouse, divorce or incarceration, through a change of personal habits or recreation, to receiving a parking ticket. The advantage of this approach is that it demonstrates the immense range of pressure factors, both in a work setting and beyond it.

Its major disadvantage, however, is that it gives the misleading impression that stress is objective and measurable. It ignores the subjective dimension of the individual's response to pressure. In short, it confuses stress with pressure.

Hopson (1984) refers to the Holmes and Rahe scale in his discussion of 'transitions'. He argues that all changes (or 'transitions') involve some degree of stress or pressure but particularly when such changes are: 'unpredictable, involuntary, unfamiliar, of high magnitude (degree of change), and high intensity (rate of change)' (p. 140).

Modern social work is, of course, awash with changes due to a flood of new legislation, other political changes and the current fashion for reorganisation (Hickson *et al.*, 1986). On this basis, we could expect to see a high level of stress in relation to the question of change in social work.

We should also be mindful of the environmental stress factors such as noise, overcrowding, poor facilities and so on. Apparently simple matters such as a lack of adequate parking facilities can raise levels of frustration and anger and once again 'up the stress stakes'. For social workers, financial stringencies have heightened what has always tended to be a sore point – albeit with many exceptions – that of poor working conditions.

These physical characteristics of the occupational environment are often not fully taken into account as a source of stress – and yet our senses are continually bombarded by stimuli originating from the environment. Adams (1980) has found that variables such as poor lighting or building layout, in combination with routinised, repetitive and dehumanising work practices lead to reduced resistance to illness. In some cases, these factors can contribute to the development of stress-related illnesses.

McDerment (1988) suggests that these issues also apply in relation to residential and day care staff when she comments that: 'We seem insensitive to the environment as a powerful tool and ally' (p. 50). Much the same can also be said of field social workers. They often have to work in cramped and poorly-designed offices which make the completion of administrative duties difficult. Such poor surroundings can prove stressful for client and worker alike, especially if interviews concerning sensitive matters have to be carried out in very unsuitable conditions, offering little privacy or constant interruptions.

In addition, both Fineman (1985) and our own study (Stress in Social Work Research Group) found that 'client unchangeability' proved to be a stressor for many social workers. The lack of success in promoting positive change acted as an additional pressure.

Finally, before moving on to coping methods, there is one set of stressors we should not forget, especially as anti-discriminatory practice is now gaining due recognition, namely sexual and racial harassment. Edelwich and Brodsky (1980) identify sexism as a contributory factor in burnout and to this we should also add racism or any other form of discriminatory or oppressive practice. (In relation to sexism, see also Cabinet Office, 1987. For issues of race and racism, see the Open University personal interest pack: 'Racism in the Workplace and Community'.) Issues of discrimination and oppression are addressed more fully in Chapter 4.

Coping methods

The effects of stress upon us will be governed not only by the level of pressure experienced, but also by the coping methods we subsequently utilise in an attempt to deal with it. Similarly, in order to prevent stress each of us develops a repertoire of coping methods.

Broadly speaking, 'coping' can be seen to occur at four levels by:

1. Removing the stressors from our lives.
2. Not allowing 'neutral' events to become stressors.
3. Developing a proficiency in dealing with situations we do not wish to avoid.

4. Seeking diversion from the pressure(s) or by relaxation (Tache and Selye, 1978).

Furthermore, it has been noted by Cox (1987) that: 'the quality of life is dependent on the ability to adjust to or cope with a wide range of . . . demands, both psychological and physical' (p. 6). In short, how well we cope with pressure depends partly on how well we are equipped – in terms of skills, strategies and resources for coping – for dealing with such pressure.

Various forms of 'diversionary' techniques are used to ward off stress. Most of these are 'spontaneous' such as long-standing hobbies or interests, going for a long walk, listening to music and so on. Others are more deliberate strategies specifically geared towards relaxation, for example, breathing exercises, biofeedback, meditation and so on. These are important pressure release valves, although many people trivialise such activities and thus undervalue the part they can play. In particular, busy social workers face this temptation as they get wrapped up in their over-full worlds. Taking time out, and knowing when to take time out, are therefore important strategies for coping.

If, as was argued earlier, stress occurs when pressure is at an inappropriate level, the subjective dimension needs to be considered. Why is a certain level of pressure perceived as inappropriate? This question of perception and 'cognitive frameworks' is particularly relevant to our understanding of coping methods. Argyle (1989) comments on how people can be helped to cope with stress by reinterpreting the situation in a more positive way:

> employees are shown that a lot of their stress is due to the way in which they perceive and interpret situations, and taught that stressful situations can be seen in less threatening ways. For example, instead of reacting to overload by feeling incompetent, workers could blame the supervisor for mismanaging the work allocation (pp. 279–80).

On this basis, it can be seen that a positive attitude is an advantage whilst low self-esteem or a tendency to blame oneself is a distinct disadvantage in terms of coping with stress and pressure. This is an example of 'cognitive restructuring' and it illustrates that stress is not only a function of objective pressure but also of subjective responses to such pressures. This subjective dimension is a key dimension of 'attribution theory', an approach which also emphasises the phenomenological dimension of cognitive and perceptual frameworks – the 'lenses' through which we view the world. Totman (1990) describes therapeutic work based on attribution theory in the following terms: 'The essence of these therapies is that someone (the therapist) injects meaning into someone else's (the client's) life using professional techniques to change attitudes about the self' (p. 174). It is a case of changing subjective attitudes or 'attributions' in order to promote a more positive, constructive – and thus less stressed – outlook.

Practitioners therefore need to be sensitive to both the subjective and objective dimensions if they are to be able to cope effectively with pressure. Similarly, managers need to take both aspects into account if they are to be successful in preventing pressure being experienced as harmful stress.

A related concept which also features in the attribution theory literature is that of 'control' or, more specifically, the 'locus of control'. It is argued that perceived control over important areas of one's life is an important part of coping with pressures and stress. The 'locus' of control can be seen as either internal, in which case we have a positive view of how much control we have over our circumstances, or external, in which case we tend to attribute events to factors beyond our control and thus marginalise the part we play in determining our own circumstances. Andrisani and Nestel (1976) show 'internals' to be more successful in work, in terms of pay, promotion and job satisfaction, compared with their 'external' counterparts. Individuals who see themselves as having more control over their lives are therefore more likely to cope with the pressures they face.

Davison and Neale (1986) also discuss the relevance of control. They comment on the work of S. C. Thompson (1981) which reviews the research on the links between stress and control. A central concept which emerges is that of 'meaning': 'In an effort to synthesise the research and theorising of others, Thompson focuses on the meaning that suffering has for individuals. If people can view a setback or an illness as part of a grand plan . . . they can place it in some meaningful perspective and endure it' (p. 133).

This further emphasises the significance of the subjective/interpretive dimension. Control, or self-control, is linked to what we are trying to achieve, to our goals in life and thus to meaning. Control is also one of the three elements in Kobasa's (1979) approach to understanding stress. She introduces the concept of 'hardiness', that is, the ability to develop resistance to stress. She sees hardiness in terms of three components:

- commitment
- control
- challenge

Kobasa and Puccetti (1983) explain this as follows:

Hardiness is defined as a constellation of three personality characteristics – commitment, control and challenge . . . Persons high in hardiness easily commit themselves to what they are doing (rather than feeling alienated), generally believe they can at least partially control events (rather than feeling powerless) and regard change to be a normal challenge or impetus to development (rather than a threat) (p. 840, quoted in Davison and Neale, 1986, pp. 170–1).

In terms of coping methods, the component parts of hardiness – commitment, control and challenge – have a significant part to play. Commitment and challenge are generally not in short supply in social work, but control can be something of a dirty word because of its associations with social control and thus with the common criticism that social workers are not 'helpers' but merely thinly disguised agents of social control. This is a problem which needs to be overcome as control is clearly a key part of stress management. It is a point to which we return in Chapter 7.

A common coping method which is something of a mixed blessing is that of 'routinisation'. As Handy (1985) points out: 'Routines are a way of coping with stress' (p. 337). Routines can be an effective and efficient way of managing our pressures but they can, of course, also stifle creativity and innovation (Kanter, 1983). They can be part of a process of retrenchment in which we risk over-reliance on previously successful coping strategies. Thus, as Atkinson *et al.* (1983) point out: 'In times of stress, people tend to resort to behaviour patterns that have worked in the past. The cautious person may become even more cautious and withdraw entirely; the aggressive person may lose control and strike out heedlessly in all directions' (p. 438).

Routines and retrenchment are concepts which exemplify Toffler's (1970) notion of 'stability zones'. However pressurised or subject to change our lives may be, we have certain areas which are constant, reassuring and help us to relax and recharge our batteries. Relationships, activities, possessions, organisations can all act as 'stability zones' and help to buffer us from stress.

A further approach to coping is that of the personality style and trait theorists. This approach assumes that coping is primarily a characteristic of the person and variations of the stressful situation are of comparatively little importance. A considerable body of research is used to support the view that the coping strategies we use will be determined by our personal traits or styles of dealing with the stressful situation (for example, 'Type A', characterised by competitiveness, aggressiveness and urgency or 'Type B', characterised by calmness and quiet confidence). These points are discussed further in Chapter 3.

This represents the view that we do not approach each coping context anew but instead carry with us a preferred set of coping strategies that remain relatively fixed across time and circumstance. Whilst appealing in some ways, this approach has been criticised by various theorists, mainly on the grounds that a person would be locked into one model of responding, thus making him or her rigid and unable to cope with a range of variations of circumstance (Folkman and Lazarus, 1980; Folkman *et al.*, 1986).

There are also gender differences to consider in relation to the psychology of coping. In their study of coping strategies, Weintraub *et al.* (1989) found significant differences in the strategies used by women and men. They found that women tended to focus on and vent emotions, as well as seek social support both for instrumental and emotional reasons, to a far greater extent than did men. In our study we found differences in emotion-focused coping, as shown in Table 2.1, though we found no significant differences between male and female social workers in seeking support from colleagues.

Table 2.1   *Gender differences in emotion-focused coping*

	'Usually' or 'All the time'	
	Male (%)	Female (%)
I let my feelings out in some way	31	47
I kept my feelings to myself	42	26
I talked to someone about how I was feeling	41	66
I talked to someone who could do something about the problem	33	55

Weintraub *et al.* also found that men tended to use negative coping strategies such as the use of alcohol and drugs far more so than women (see the discussion below of 'negative coping'). They suggest that differences in coping styles need not necessarily be linked to personality *per se*. In their view: 'people tend to adopt certain coping tactics as relatively stable preferences. Stable preferences may derive from personality or they may develop for other reasons' (p. 270). Thus, we cannot totally discount personality as a contributing factor to our coping abilities, although this facet does appear to have been overstated in much of the literature on stress and coping. (The role of personality will be discussed more fully in Chapter 3 and issues of gender, along with other social divisions, in Chapter 4.)

With regard specifically to the coping methods used by social workers, Fineman (1985) found that the dominant style of coping used was an internalisation of difficulties, a 'building up' of anxiety in the hope that it would disappear spontaneously or could be released elsewhere. Some workers later reworked their anxiety, that is, re-appraised the situation, whilst others projected their anxiety onto others.

In her study of social workers, Satyamurti (1981) found that the coping strategies most commonly used ranged from the protective response 'it could happen to anyone', to specific avoidance behaviours such as diverting attention elsewhere, seeking promotion, taking unofficial time off, or even to the extreme of resigning. A prevalent coping strategy used was that of 'defensive distancing'. This led to social workers using language which categorised clients as helpless, immature and recalcitrant, an example of the 'depersonalisation' associated with burnout.

In a study of residential and day care workers McDerment (1988) found that the most commonly reported way of coping was to switch off and try to come to terms with situations as they arose. She found that individual diversion techniques included a wide range of activities: meditation, yoga, gardening, painting, praying, reading, cooking, baking and various sporting activities.

There is a vast array of literature advising the individual on ways to cope. Suggestions include the utilisation of self-management skills, transcendental meditation, relaxation, and physical exercise. There are of course very many other coping skills, methods and strategies above and beyond the ones mentioned here (see the discussions in Chapter 3). However, having outlined some of the major methods and issues, there is one significant point which needs to be made about the use of such methods before we move on to examine support systems.

The point relates to the success or otherwise of some coping methods. That is, there are some methods which, although they may be successful in the short term, do more harm than good. For example, Freud wrote of unsuccessful defence mechanisms such as 'denial' (Freud, 1933). In the short term, we pretend a problem does not exist but, because of this denial, it hits us all the harder in the long run. Similarly, drinking to excess may be useful occasionally but, as we saw in Chapter 1, as an habitual strategy it is fraught with obvious dangers. Inappropriate application of coping methods (or 'negative coping') may therefore cause an escalation of stress and ultimately bring about a crisis. (This is a key aspect of crisis theory and the therapeutic approach of crisis intervention – see Caplan, 1961; Thompson, 1991b.) In our study we found that those who typically used emotional venting showed slightly, but significantly, less distress, while those who tended to brood on the problem and blame themselves reported considerably more distress.

Practice Focus 2.2

Sylvia became manager at the day centre when the previous occupant of the post took early retirement. Her predecessor had been a very popular leader and the staff were very sorry to see her go. They also seemed to resent the fact that the deputy manager, who was also very popular, had not been promoted to manager. She therefore found herself in a very difficult position in her first managerial post. When her deputy began to undermine her, it soon became clear that the staff were 'taking sides'– against her rather than for her.

Sylvia was understandably extremely upset by this and experienced the whole affair as very stressful. The situation persisted for quite some time and proved increasingly difficult to tolerate. Sylvia coped very well at first but with time her resolve grew weak and she began to rely more and more on alcohol. She soon entered a classic cycle of negative coping. Her drinking became more of a problem than a solution – and she gradually got to the stage where drinking was the only way she could cope. Drinking became a vicious circle in which her coping repertoire was reduced to a single method, and a destructive one at that.

In sum, coping methods are crucial in resisting stress and so the development and expansion of a repertoire of helpful coping methods (and a sensitivity to the dangers of unhelpful or inappropriate methods) is something that all social workers should pursue and which all managers should encourage and facilitate. Indeed, it is crucial to note that managers have a dual responsibility in this respect, first, to facilitate coping in others and, second, to ensure that they themselves are developing appropriate strategies for coping with their own pressures.

Support systems

This is the oft-neglected third dimension of our theoretical model. Much of the traditional literature on stress ignores or marginalises the question of support. Stress management is seen as a set of techniques for steeling oneself against occupational and life stresses. However, to put it somewhat bluntly and cynically, techniques such as breathing exercises and a better diet are of little use if workers are exposed to extreme and intense pressures without adequate support or backing. Certainly diet, exercise and so on are important parts of the equation but they are no substitute for strong and effective support. What support systems are, or should be, available is the topic to which we now turn.

Support systems can be divided into two categories, formal and informal. Formal support is available, in theory at least, via line management supervision and consultation (Brown, 1984), appraisal systems (Randell *et al.*, 1984), and other such human resource management functions (Torrington and Hall, 1988). As many of the stressors outlined earlier relate to organisational/managerial issues, for example role stress, it follows that managers have a not insignificant part to play in supporting workers by 'manipulating the variables' of work pressures.

Formal support can be subdivided into two categories as follows:

1. *Preventative.* Ensuring that staff are not overloaded, that expectations are clear and that adequate consultation and supervision are provided – these are all prophylactic support measures: they are proactive. In our study, only

49 per cent of social workers agreed with the statement: 'My line manager fully appreciates the stressors of my job', and only 48 per cent reported that: 'After supervision I feel less stressed', while 11 per cent reported that unrealistically high expectations by their immediate supervisor caused them 'considerable' or 'extreme' stress.

2. *Reactive.* Preventative measures relate to dealing with pressure in terms of preventing it from spilling over into stress. However, when such measures fail, as is often the case in such a demanding vocation as social work, additional steps need to be taken to ensure that support systems are effective. These include offering or arranging appropriate counselling (Megranahan, 1983), arranging or facilitating 'time-out' or perhaps joint work.

One aspect of support which cuts across both preventative and reactive elements is that of 'ethos' – a supportive atmosphere or climate. Managers, and other staff, have a responsibility for creating or maintaining a team or work-base which recognises the pressures, encourages the open expression of feelings and discourages a 'macho' culture (Wiener, 1989) which blames or 'pathologises' workers for wanting or needing support. As Arroba and James put it: 'Organisations which rely on survival of the fittest not only wreak havoc in people's lives but also fail to create a climate conducive to success. Managing pressure and reducing stress is not an optional extra for managers' (1987, p. xvi).

Formal support is therefore a very significant area for managers. In effect, such support is doubly important, for without it, social workers will not only be less well-equipped to cope with the inherent pressures of the job, they will also experience such a lack of support as constituting a significant pressure in itself. Therefore, we can see that there is no neutral ground for managers in terms of formal support. If a manager is not helping, then he or she is surely hindering, as a lack of formal support is likely to be interpreted in terms of the following:

- a lack of security or 'safety-net'
- a feeling of being undervalued

- a generally low level of morale
- a possible resentment of managers 'not earning their pay'

When the actions or attitudes of managers contribute to producing such a situation, the level of pressure is increased, rather than decreased. This is represented diagrammatically in Figure 2.2.

Figure 2.2 *Management support*

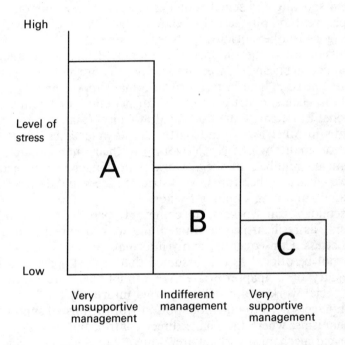

The impact of failing to provide formal support is therefore not simply that between level C and level B but, more realistically, that between level C and level A. The cost of neglecting such support functions should therefore be abundantly clear – a significant issue when we consider that, in our study across three local authorities, 39 per cent of social workers indicated that they 'did not receive as much supervision as they should'.

Informal support also has a significant role to play. There are two main categories of support: within the work setting and without. Within work, there are such helpful, pressure-relieving factors as peer support, camaraderie, professional fellowship and so on. In our study, social workers who agreed with the statements: 'I can discuss difficult situations with my colleagues' and 'I can depend upon my colleagues for practical support' reported lower levels of distress. Also of import are shared sporting and social activities and, of course, humour – 51 per cent of our sample believed that: 'Socialising with colleagues is a beneficial way to reduce stress.'

Outside work, the support of the family, friends and other social contacts can often be drawn upon. However, there is a significant issue here in terms of informal support and social workers; such support may not be forthcoming for two main reasons. First, partly due to 'social mobility' (that is, moving to jobs in other areas) and partly due to reluctance, on the part of many workers, to work on their 'home patch', significant numbers of social workers no longer live in their native areas and therefore have restricted access to the support of family and long-standing friends.

Second, social workers are commonly perceived as 'good copers', as resilient people trained and well-equipped to deal with stress. Consequently, many informal sources of support may not be offered as it is assumed that such support is not necessary or is inappropriate. We cannot therefore assume that social workers are well supported informally.

Managers need to take note not only of the formal support mechanisms, where they have direct control, but also of the informal mechanisms which are indirectly related to management. Managers may have little control over informal support measures but knowing what support is available for staff and promoting such support where possible, can be seen as worthwhile tactics to pursue. The importance of support is emphasised by many others. For example, Hopson (1984) comments that: 'interpersonal warmth and support during stressful periods seems to reduce the impact of the stress' (p. 140).

Also, Wiener (1989) links together issues of formal and informal support:

> Support is particularly important before and after difficult incidents or sessions. Support also prevents stresses at home and at work reinforcing each other. If there are no means at the end of the day for letting go of the feelings that have been churned up, then workers end up turning the people they live with into unpaid counsellors (p. 20).

And, finally, Gibson *et al.*, reporting on an empirical study of stress in social work, comment that: 'Social workers' most frequently reported wish was for more appreciation from their managers' (1989, p. 17).

A number of writers (for example, Cooper and Marshall, 1976) have suggested that organisations can play a significant role in reducing stressors in their environments and in augmenting, supporting and developing the capacity of individuals to deal with occupational stress. The organisation can act at three levels to achieve these aims:

1. The organisational level.
2. The work group/team level.
3. The individual level.

The organisation can – and, we would argue, should – act in both preventative and remedial ways, the ideal being to maximise 'person–environment fit' (Argyle, 1989). Such action may lead to changes in policies, the development of support networks and greater access to training. However, many social work organisations have not taken these issues of staff care seriously. For example, it took the death of a social worker in the course of her duties to spur Birmingham Social Services into positively promoting staff welfare on a large scale. Part of this strategy included the employment of a full-time stress counsellor.

But, even when support services are offered on an 'in house' basis, the take up rate may be very low as staff can be very mistrustful of how the organisation will perceive the situation. When a confidential telephone 'Helpline' was offered to 3000 staff employed in five London Social Services and Probation Departments, Hemsley (1986) reported that only eight responses were received over one year and only one of these concerned work-related stress. The Burnout Study and Support Group (1986) suggested that staff support groups were the most favoured means of acceptable assistance.

Support is a factor which the majority of people would intuitively identify as being important in coping with pressures and avoiding stress. Payne (1980) defines support as: 'the degree to which the environment makes available resources (natural, physical, intellectual, financial and social) relevant to the demands made upon the system (person, group or organisation)' (p. 284). Social support has been identified as a resource that helps people cope with job stress through supportive relationships with others (House, 1981). Various studies have shown how a positive relationship with family, friends and co-workers can offset many of the effects of pressure and stress (Gore, 1978). For example, George (1989) argues that: 'there is general agreement that social support is multidimensional and substantial consensus that different dimensions of support vary in importance for different outcomes' (p. 247). For example, informal support often plays a major role in an employed person's occupational life. People in employment often cite their families as one of the most important emotional resources for coping with job pressures (Crouter, 1984).

Caplan (1967) highlighted the importance of the family. He suggested that the family served a number of different functions for the individual:

- a collector of information about the world
- a feedback/guidance system
- a source of ideology
- a guide and mediator in problem solving
- a source of practical service and aid
- a haven for rest and recuperation
- a reference and control group

It is therefore not surprising that he saw the work group as a less important influence than the family as the former is likely to have far less knowledge about the person and his or her needs.

Guteck *et al.* (1988) note that, if we review the studies where married couples are asked to describe the kind of work-related support that spouses provide, the most commonly cited is that of listening and offering advice about how to handle a problematic situation, which, ironically, is one of the expectations of good practice in social work supervision.

One of the ways in which support from the family reduces job pressures is in an indirect or 'buffering' manner (Cohen and Willis, 1985). Thus the amount of support received from our families will have a direct effect on how we are affected by occupational pressures. For example, Berkowitz and Perkins (1984) found that the more support a woman received from her husband, the weaker were her feelings of being overloaded with conflicting job and family role demands. Similarly, Guteck *et al.* (1988) provide evidence to suggest that women are better providers of both instrumental and emotional support than men.

Whilst support from the family is usually positive, it should be noted that it can also have a very negative effect by encouraging ineffective coping strategies, or by collusion with defence-avoidance behaviours, that is, behaviours that avoid problems rather than tackle them head on. Such behaviour will not only fail to help to deal with existing problems but are likely to add to existing pressures, thereby possibly producing a worse situation.

The family can also, of course, be a major source of pressure in itself due to relationship difficulties, communication problems or other conflicts, as is made clear by the family therapy literature (Barker, 1986; Kirschner and Kirschner, 1986). Laing (1971) and others even go so far as to argue that the family is a major source of mental disorder due to its often conflicting and contradictory demands (Thompson, 1991c).

Colleagues can also be a significant source of support. For example, Cooper *et al.* (1988) argue that for many: 'their co-workers act as a substitute family group' (p. 72). Lazarus (1966) suggested that supportive social relationships with peers, supervisors, and subordinates at work are less likely to create interpersonal pressures and will directly reduce the level of perceived job stress. Co-worker support is especially important before or after a stressful incident. Support helps the worker verbalise a lot of his or her internal fears and concerns and this, in itself, makes them less threatening. The mere knowledge that support is available makes workers more confident and willing to take chances as they will feel better equipped to deal with potentially stressful situations.

Of course, managers have a central role to play as far as support is concerned. For example, Buck (1972) found that when a manager is perceived as being 'considerate', he or she is seen as being respected, trustworthy, and warm. Alternatively, when workers perceived their line manager as being low on consideration, they complained of:

- feeling under pressure
- not receiving enough feedback
- the manager playing 'favourites', and other power games

Style of management is obviously an important aspect of social work primarily because of its effect on others within the organisation. Whilst different situations may call for a different type of management, the literature would suggest that a more democratic, human-relations oriented leadership is usually the most effective (Fielder, 1967).

Managers can be the source of several types of support (Cherniss, 1980):

1. *Advice*. They can suggest more effective ways of dealing with a problem.
2. *Sounding boards*. Staff should be able to ventilate their feelings or discuss new ideas with their line manager.
3. *Feedback*. Line managers should be a source of praise as well as constructive criticism.
4. *Information*. Staff should be able to obtain relevant information regarding work tasks plus information regarding policy, goals and other activities related to the organisation.
5. *Buffer and advocate*. Line managers can often be seen as allies. As managers have enhanced organisational power

they are usually in a better position to buffer external organisational stressors.

Overall, however, the most important function of a manager is that of being responsive to his or her staff's needs, as an organisation which pays inadequate attention to its human resources is an organisation which is storing up problems for itself.

Conclusion

A number of concepts have been introduced here in order to provide an overview of the main areas of knowledge in relation to stress and stress management. The exposition is, of course, by no means exhaustive but is, we hope, sufficient to stimulate further debate, discussion and study. The concepts have been presented as part of a three-dimensional theoretical framework, encompassing stressors, coping methods and support systems. This framework is presented as a useful model to act as a foundation for understanding stress issues. The framework is summarised in Figure 2.3.

Well-developed coping methods and support systems reduce the impact of stressors whilst poorly developed resistance can prove ineffective at best, or seriously magnify the pressure at worst. It is clear from Figure 2.3 that reducing the human and financial costs of stress depends on facilitating and promoting the development of strong and effective support systems and coping methods. The two aspects, coping and support, exist in symbiosis (for example, good support raises confidence and enhances coping skills). Thus, good support tends to engender good coping methods and poor support adds to the strain on coping resources.

There are a number of managerial and practice implications to be drawn from this framework. Consequently, the ideas and issues raised here are intended as 'food for thought' to help and to encourage social work staff to develop a strategy for alleviating and preventing stress. These implications can be summarised as follows:

Figure 2.3   *The theoretical framework*

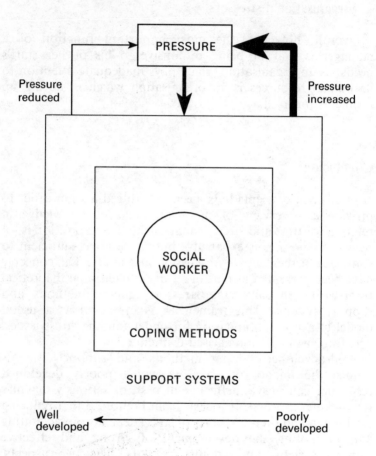

Source: Thompson (1991b).

- many of the common causes of stress are to be found in social work
- stress is a significant source of staffing problems in social work (NALGO, 1989)
- social work personnel are generally seen as 'resilient'; care needs to be taken to acknowledge the pressure and prevent a build-up by encouraging an outlet; the notion of

'resilience' can make such an outlet seem unnecessary, and therefore add to the pressure

- stress is not simply an objective matter of pressure but also a subjective matter of how workers interpret or appraise such pressure and how they respond to it; managers can play a helpful role in respect of both the objective and subjective aspects
- effective support systems are essential if the human, professional and financial costs of stress are to be minimised

In short, supporting staff in coping with pressure is a key managerial function. 38 per cent of the social workers in our study reported that: 'My line manager could provide better quality supervision' and these workers were more likely to report job-related distress. The slogan 'People Matter' will therefore remain an empty cliché if stress and stress management are not high on both the management and professional practice agendas. This raises a number of practical points for social work staff who are seeking the most effective means of dealing with stress. We shall return to, and highlight, many of these issues in each of the following chapters.

3

Stress, Coping and Personality

Introduction

Using the Arroba and James definition of stress as 'your response to an inappropriate level of pressure' (1987, p. 3), we can see that the psychological make-up of the individual is going to have a significant bearing on the experience of stress. Stress is not simply an inappropriate level of pressure, it is our *response* to that pressure. That is, there is a significant subjective dimension that needs to be considered if our understanding of stress is to be anything other than superficial. How we perceive pressures, what coping responses we use and what support systems apply will depend, to a large extent, on personality factors. This chapter will therefore explore the issues of personality that can be seen to play a part in the management of pressure and stress.

The chapter covers two broad areas. First, we shall review some of the most common approaches to personality theory and consider how they apply to issues of stress. Second, we shall examine the characteristic personality factors and coping responses relevant to social workers and social work practice. By tackling the subject matter in this way we are covering the broader context of personality theory and stress before moving on to explore the specific question of how such factors have an impact on the experience of stress in social work. We shall begin with what is probably the best known, and certainly one of the most influential, approaches to personality theory, that of psychodynamics.

Psychodynamics

Psychodynamic theory owes much to the extensive writings of Sigmund Freud and the many theorists who have built on the foundations laid by his psychoanalytical approach. Space does not permit a detailed account of even the basics of psychodynamic theory and so we shall restrict ourselves to a brief outline of some of the key aspects of this approach to personality development.

Freud is perhaps best known for his twofold emphasis on sexuality and the unconscious. He depicted human psychology in terms of a conflict between the sexual drive ('libido') and social mores which forbade the open expression of sexual desire. He described this conflict in terms of a three-part model of the person – the 'id', 'ego' and 'superego'. The id represents the irrational forces of libido which are largely hidden from consciousness. The superego, by contrast, represents our conscience, the internalisation of rules and values passed on to us through socialisation. These two forces are often in conflict. The personal, selfish id clashes with the superego which demands sacrifice of personal desires and feelings in favour of the social good, in favour of what Freud called 'civilisation'. This is where the ego comes in. The ego is the rational controller, the 'mediator' of conflicting forces. As such, the ego's task is to balance the demands of the id against those of the superego.

Where this balance is not satisfactorily achieved, stress can result. For example, if the id is dominant, the ensuing irrational and selfish actions can lead to considerable social disapproval, sanctions and so on. Where the superego is dominant, considerable guilt and self-repression can sap confidence and give rise to a great deal of anxiety. In psychodynamic terms, stress management can be seen as a process of achieving a healthy balance between the id and the superego.

Part of achieving this balance is the use of 'defence mechanisms', processes whereby external threats to the ego can be deflected. These mechanisms can be positive and constructive as, for example, when sexual energy is 'sublimated' or rechannelled into more socially acceptable forms such as sport, work or hobbies. They can also be negative and destructive as, for example, when 'denial' is used to pretend that the threat or problem does not exist.

The main criticism levelled at psychoanalytic personality theories is their vagueness and apparent lack of scientific validity; that is, they are not easily testable, although Kline (1972) has claimed that Freud's basic propositions can, if suitably modified, be made accessible to empirical investigation. However, even with the supposed methodological problems regarding the verification of psychoanalytic procedures, Hobfall (1988) contends that stress research has never disproved the psychoanalytic model but has simply 'sidestepped the issue' (p. 48).

Behaviourism

The behaviourist approach to personality is based on the principles of 'learning theory'. All behaviour is said to be learned by conditioning and reinforcement, by a process of learning which behaviours produce a positive response and which do not. One of the major proponents of behaviourism is B. F. Skinner who held that behaviour is determined by instrumental, or 'operant', conditioning. The main foundation of this model is that an antecedent event (A) occurs which produces a behaviour (B) which has consequences (C). According to this model, it is up to each of us to manage the link, or contingency, between our actions and outcomes in order to produce as many positive consequences as possible (see Figure 3.1).

Where such patterns of behaviour are appropriate to the situation we will be able to cope with the pressures we face. However, if we have learned patterns of behaviour which are not appropriate to the situations we find ourselves in, then stress is the likely outcome. Stress management, in behaviourist terms, is therefore seen as a process of learning new and

Figure 3.1   *The ABC of behaviour*

more appropriate behaviours so that our actions can succeed in achieving positive, rather than negative consequences.

Social learning theory

Rotter (1954) classified individuals according to the degree to which an internal or external locus of control was reflected in their behaviour (see Chapter 2). In a later work (Rotter, 1966) he argued that people with either an extreme internal or external locus of control score had a higher probability of being 'maladjusted' psychologically than those scoring in the middle range. More significantly for our purposes, research has shown that those who have an internal locus of control are more able to withstand pressures (Johnstone and Sarason, 1978; Sancler and Lakey, 1982).

Rotter was also one of the first theorists to develop a 'social learning theory' approach. He argued that the sources of reinforcement are related to beliefs about whether internal or external forces are responsible for what happens to us. Such beliefs will affect how we behave in any given situation. According to Rotter, behaviour is guided by our response to factors in the environment that can be seen to offer satisfaction of needs. Past events are important in so far as they provide a blueprint for us as to how we should behave in order to obtain a reward. Similarly, future events are crucial to the extent that we have expectations as to what actions will maximise reward. According to this theory, it may therefore be possible to predict a person's response to any given situation, if we are aware of:

- what he or she has previously learned
- what his or her expectations are
- what aspects of the environment provide the most satisfying rewards (Rotter and Hochreich, 1975)

Modern social learning theorists, whilst still emphasising the importance of the environment, have also started to realise the role of 'cognition', the psychological processes of receiving, and making sense of, information. Thus, aspects of the individual, the environment, and the interaction between the two, are seen as playing a major role in personality development.

One of the more progressive social learning theories is that put forward by Bandura (1977). According to Bandura, an individual may acquire a wide range of responses by modelling the behaviour of others. We may therefore learn to deal with a stressful situation by observing how others cope with the situation. Indeed, this is the major implication of the social learning theory approach to stress – we cope with pressures by learning appropriate strategies for interacting with the social environment.

Humanistic psychology

The basic underlying concept of humanistic psychology is that people are fundamentally 'good'; that is, our orientation towards others and to the world is primarily a positive and well-meaning one. Evil or destructive actions or events arise as a result of the distortion, repression or frustration of this basic goodness. For example, people who are afforded little or no respect or self-esteem will not value themselves and, therefore, are unlikely to value others. Consequently, the aim of humanistic psychology is to understand and remove these barriers to, and distortions of, the underlying natural goodness.

Owing much to the work of writers such as Abraham Maslow and Carl Rogers, the humanistic approach is one which emphasises the need for personal growth and self-actualisation. And this is where issues of stress become relevant as the frustration of this need for self-actualisation is likely to be experienced as stressful. For social work clients, factors such as poverty, inadequate housing or ill-health can act as significant barriers to such personal growth. They can therefore be experienced as 'double stressors' – a source of pressure in their own right *and* obstacles to self-actualisation. A parallel situation can be seen to exist for social work staff in terms of the 'barriers' of inadequate resources, poor working environments and so on.

But humanistic psychology is not just about the 'objective' factors that hamper personal growth. It is also about the subjective dimension of meaning, purpose and values – factors identified in Chapter 1 as important aspects of understanding, and dealing with, pressure and stress. Payne (1991) comments that humanistic (and existential) models:

> have in common ideas that human beings are trying to make sense of the world that they experience, that social workers are trying to help people gain the skills to explore themselves and the personal meaning that they attach to the world they perceive and which affects them, and that their interpretations of their own selves are valid and worthwhile (p. 169).

As we noted in Chapter 1, both the subjective and objective dimensions of pressure and stress need to be taken into account. The humanist perspective therefore has advantages in this respect.

Payne goes on to comment on the work of Carkhuff and Berenson (1977) who describe five themes that characterise humanistic psychologies and therapies. These are:

- we can only understand ourselves in relation to others
- our main anxiety in life is losing others and being alone
- we are guilty because we cannot achieve a creative life
- we alone have responsibility to act on our decisions
- therapy aims to help us act and accept freedom and responsibility in doing so (Payne, 1991, p. 171)

In humanistic terms, therefore, stress derives from the frustration of human potential and so stress management should be geared towards identifying and, as far as possible, removing obstacles to achieving meaning, fulfilment and self-respect.

Existentialism

The existentialist approach to personality is broadly similar to that of humanistic psychology. It emphasises the importance of finding meaning, value and purpose in our lives and recognises existence as a striving towards this. However, it differs from humanism in a number of key ways, as the following two examples show:

- Existentialism does not see people as primarily 'good'; rather, we are inherently neither good nor evil. How we act depends not on an underlying nature or 'essence', but rather on our *choices* – our 'choice of being'.
- Although humanistic psychology takes some account of wider social factors, its focus remains primarily at the level of the individual. Existentialism, by contrast, pays much fuller attention to the 'sociopolitical context' (Thompson, 1992a) in which individual actions are located.

These two differences are both enshrined within the following passage:

Existentialism is a philosophy which places human freedom at the forefront of its attempts to understand the various dimensions of existence. But this is no easy freedom, no caprice or idealism. It is a freedom grounded in the myriad constraints, influences and sober lessons of complex social and political interactions. It is a freedom which entails responsibility, ownership of one's actions and their consequences. Such freedom is both a heavy burden and the key to overcoming a range of problems of our own making – self-made barriers to deny freedom and responsibility at both an individual and collective level.

The existentialist portrayal of humanity is of people seeking to make sense of an absurd existence, located within a broader context of structured inequalities and the oppression and alienation they engender. It is argued that the problems social workers face have a significant existential dimension and . . . an approach informed by the tenets of existentialism is necessary to do justice to this complex subject (Thompson, 1992a, p. vii).

Existentialism therefore shares with humanism the notion that seeking meaning and purpose are important aspects of dealing with pressure and stress. However, existentialist theorists would go a step further and argue that a key part of stress management must be to seek 'authentic' existence – a way of life that helps us come to terms with the heavy burden of personal responsibility for our actions and the realisation that life affords us little certainty or security (Thompson, 1992b).

Type and trait theories

This approach is premised on the belief that we have certain stable characteristics or patterns of behaviour that influence how we deal with social situations, including those that involve pressure and stress. These patterns are known as 'traits' and are felt to be relatively constant over time and across various situations, for example, shyness or aggressiveness. As Atkinson *et al.* (1983) put it:

The *trait approach* to personality attempts to isolate and describe the basic properties of the individual that direct behaviour . . . Trait theories assume that people vary on a number of personality *dimensions*, or *scales*, each of which represents a *trait*. Thus, we could rate an individual on a scale of intelligence, emotional stability, aggressiveness and so on. To arrive at a global description of personality, we would need to know how the individual is rated on a number of dimensions (pp. 388–9).

Where such traits are clustered together, psychologists would use the term 'personality type', that is, a relatively stable and consistent pattern of traits. This area of study has featured as a major area of psychological research both in general terms and, more specifically, in relation to issues of pressure and stress. We shall consider briefly some of the main concepts and approaches that have proved to be influential in the stress research literature.

Personality types

Probably the most significant personality type encountered in stress theory is that of the 'Type A personality'. This is a term that dates back to the 1950s and the work of Rosenman and Friedman (1959). They found that a significant proportion of heart disease patients, particularly those below 60 years of age, displayed a consistent clustering of personality characteristics. The term 'Type A personality' was used to describe this constellation of traits:

- a sustained drive towards poorly-defined goals
- hostility and competitiveness
- a high level of ambition
- a preoccupation with work and deadlines
- irritability and a low tolerance of frustration

Practice Focus 3.1

Ian was a team leader of two years' experience. He was ambitious and, ultimately, wished to enter senior management. Two years after qualifying as a social worker he began to apply for team leader posts and was eventually successful. At interview he was keen to convince the panel that he would get the job done and, when in post, he tried to do the same – setting very high expectations of himself and his team. He expected them to be able to cope with the work, come what may.

He developed a very uneasy relationship with his team. Although always polite, there seemed to be considerable anger and criticism under the surface. He also felt annoyed when he thought his team members were consulting him too much (Why did they not get on with it?) and anxious when they did not consult him enough (Are they going behind my back?). Eventually, the team began to divide into two camps: two male social workers who identified with Ian and socialised with him, and five women workers and two male workers who avoided him wherever possible.

Ian felt stressed and did not know what to do about it. His behaviour at work became erratic and, at home, quite aggressive. He blamed it on the 'unsatisfactory' members of his team and did not understand how his unrealistic expectations had contributed to the situation.

A number of studies have supported the initial hypothesis that Type A people are more prone to heart disease (Rosenman *et al.*, 1966; Haynes and Feinleib, 1982). 'Type B' people, by contrast, do not have these characteristics and are able to unwind and relax:

Type B individuals are able to relax without feeling guilty and work without becoming agitated; they lack a sense of time urgency with its accompanying impatience. Angry and hostile feelings are not easily aroused in these individuals, and they show little need to display or discuss achievements (Atkinson *et al.*, 1983, p. 440).

Not surprisingly, no link has been drawn between Type B behaviour and heart disease. It is as if the Type A characteristics place too much strain on the body, the heart in particular, whilst the more 'laid-back' approach of Type B people causes no such strain.

Sutherland and Cooper (1991) comment that: 'there are no distinct divisions between Type A and Type B. Rather people fall somewhere on a continuum leaning more towards one type than the other' (p. 243). It is therefore a task for each of us to assess whether our behaviour is more reflective of Type A or Type B, and take corresponding action to guard against the possible negative effects.

A further development on the theme of stress-related behaviour types is the work of Braike (1986) who incorporated a gender dimension by introducing the notion of the 'Type E' woman (Type A people are predominantly, although not exclusively, male). While the Type E woman shares many of the traits of the Type A person, she experiences added pressures as a result of her gender. Such women have managed to be successful, Braike argues, by the development of such qualities as assertiveness, independence, autonomy and decisiveness. However, this can go too far as, for example, when some Type E women develop the belief that they must be 'everything to everybody' – their family, partner, and employers (Braike, 1986, p. 63). They view their own needs, for example, the need for nurturance and protection, as a weakness both in themselves and others. In order to deny their own needs, Type E women create relationships where others become dependent on them. Such relationships can be seen as a protection mechanism for such women against the pain and frustration of not having anyone to meet their needs. Type E women tend to refuse to let themselves be in a vulnerable position, or to experience a need for another person.

In the work place, Type E women are more likely to have difficulty asking for help or requesting support, and feel that they must maintain a tough image not unlike that of their Type A counterparts. Also like Type A people, they tend to be poor delegators, as this undermines their position and they will be of the belief that no one else could complete the task as well as they can. Due to her failure to communicate her needs to others, the Type E woman is 'condemned to frustration' (Braike, 1986, p. 164). As Type E women continue to try to be everything to everyone, this tends to lead to the development of more and more stress. As the demands upon her build up, she is caught in a 'cycle of efficiency'; the more she seems to be able to cope, the greater are the demands made of her. This may not only be harmful for the woman concerned, but also for those around her. Unfortunately, the Type E woman's behaviour will be sustained by many of those around her due to a covert collusion on the part of those involved. Of course, the people whose needs are met by the Type E woman will not want to 'rock the boat'.

Braike (1986) argues that the only way for women to break free from the Type E cycle is to examine their position in society and the way their social roles are constructed (this links in with our discussion of gender and sexism in Chapter 4, as there are clear connections between the notion of Type E and the patriarchal expectations of women in modern society). They also need to ensure that they reject the myth that needing to be nurtured is a sign of weakness. Finally as Braike (1986) puts it: 'The solution to excessive self-reliance is essentially a paradox. You need to be strong and self reliant in order to let yourself be vulnerable and needful of others' (p. 67).

Practice Focus 3.2

Eileen had been recognised as a very positive and successful social worker. She had moved into management at a junior level and, although she had enjoyed it, she felt constantly under pressure to 'look after' her male colleagues. On her promotion to middle management, she felt a tremendous tug between the manager she wanted to be and the manager she was expected to be. She was expected to focus on tasks, being tough, ruthless and a work-machine. Eileen's clear ability was in focusing on the person, enabling her staff to do the job and concentrating on good practice, rather than criticising bad.

Whenever, Eileen showed task focus, she was praised, her person focus being seen as 'soft'. Eileen was being torn in two directions and felt extremely stressed – should she 'join the club' or should she fight on, or even go back to a practitioner role?

Hardiness

Another key concept within the 'trait' literature is that of 'hardiness', a concept we discussed in Chapter 2. Maddi and Kobasa (1984) argue that people with what they call a 'hardy personality' will experience less stress. A 'hardy personality' is said to have:

- a high level of commitment
- an internal locus of control
- a tendency to welcome challenge

For Kobasa (1979) hardiness is a key factor in how we interpret potentially stressful life events. The notion of hardiness emphasises the importance of adopting a positive approach to the pressures we face. In particular, hardiness is characterised by seeing change as a challenge and a possibility for growth, rather than a threat to our security (Kobasa *et al.*, 1982). Clearly, this has major implications for stress management.

Locus of control

As already noted, the locus of control is another personality trait which is believed to determine how we will react in a pressurised or stressful situation. It is argued that those of us who have an 'internal locus of control' will believe we have control over what happens in our lives, and that our decisions and actions influence personal outcomes. Alternatively, those of us who have an 'external locus of control' will attribute events to factors beyond our control. In line with this, Sutherland and Cooper (1991) suggest that the locus of control may be significant in our choice of occupation. For example, internals are more likely to select jobs where a high degree of perceived control is possible.

Seligman (1975) suggests that externals are more likely to suffer from 'learned helplessness'. They are more likely to give up and withdraw in stressful situations whilst internals will attempt to cope. According to Seligman, learned helplessness will affect our motivation to act, as well as our ability to believe that we can play an active part in determining our own future. It can also lead some individuals to experience an emotional imbalance, possibly giving rise to depression, anger and anxiety. In a similar vein, Cherniss (1980) contends that learned helplessness may be the ultimate source of burnout.

Neurotic anxiety

Some degree of anxiety in certain circumstances is, of course, a 'normal' part of everyday life. However, for some people, it takes on unreasonable proportions and becomes a major feature of their lives. In such cases the term 'neurotic anxiety' tends to be used. This condition can be seen to be characterised by:

- a tendency to set oneself very high goals and adopt a punitive attitude towards oneself where these goals are not fulfilled
- emotional instability
- a very apprehensive approach to new situations
- low self-esteem and an excessive concern about the opinions of others

In our study in three local authorities, we found only 47 per cent of our sample of field social workers showing 'normal' levels of anxiety, with 25 per cent showing 'pathological' levels, and a further 28 per cent 'borderline'. Other research has shown close links between burnout in social work and health care staff and a combination of neurotic anxiety, unrealistic life goals and low self-esteem (Pines and Kafry, 1978). A proneness to anxiety is therefore a potentially serious barrier to effective stress management.

Freudenberger's classification

Freudenberger (1975) argued that there were three types of helping personality that he believed to be more likely to experience the effects of stress and burnout:

1. *The dedicated personality*. This type of person is committed to his or her work but gets overinvolved and takes too much on. According to Freudenberger, such a worker: 'feels from within himself the pressure to succeed [and] feels from without himself the pressure of the needs of the population he is trying to serve' (p. 74).
2. *The overcommitted personality*. This type of person tends to have an unsatisfactory life outside work and uses work as a 'haven'. The danger here is efforts become geared more towards meeting his or her own needs than those of service users.
3. *The authoritarian personality*. This represents: 'the type of individual who so needs to be in control that no one else can do the job as well as he can' (p. 74).

These three types are, of course, not mutually exclusive. One person may show aspects of each in differing contexts. The high levels of pressure associated with such personality types make the people concerned far more vulnerable to stress. This, in the long term, may lead to burnout and a deterioration in the level of service offered.

Indeed, this is a common feature of the trait and type theories – they all propose certain sets of characteristics that are significant with regard to how we deal with pressure and stress. However, perhaps the most significant weakness in this style of approach is that it gives the impression that such dispositions are fixed and immutable. They can therefore be seen to promote an unduly pessimistic view of the possibilities for change – they encourage a deterministic and reductionist approach to the study of personality. .

The psychology of personal identity

As a counterbalance to the deterministic tendencies implicit in many of the approaches to personality, we should remember that personal identity is a dynamic and fluid entity and constantly in a certain degree of flux. Thus, various factors such as time, context, and mood, plus a host of individual differences, will all affect how we react in potentially stressful situations. As we emphasised earlier, the subjective dimension of perception and interpretation (the phenomenological dimension) is a very important factor and one we would do well not to ignore.

Stress research has highlighted that an individual's perception is a critical factor in the stress process. In simple terms, if one does not perceive the situation as stressful, then it will not be experienced as such. Perception, in the context of stress research, has been defined as: 'the influence of cognitive processes in the assessment of environmental events, resulting in individual interpretation of the personal meaning of an event' (Hobfall, 1988, p. 97). This relates closely to the distinction, drawn in Chapter 1, between pressure and stress. The term 'stress' becomes applicable when pressures are perceived or experienced as harmful.

Echoing a similar sentiment, Folkman *et al.* (1986) comment that: 'cognitive appraisal is a process through which the person evaluates whether a particular encounter with the environment is relevant to his or her well-being, and if so in what ways' (p. 992). In 'primary' appraisal we evaluate whether or not anything is at stake, whilst in 'secondary' appraisal we decide what, if anything, can be done to prevent or overcome harm.

The role of values is another important factor that has been highlighted in relation to the interaction of personality and stress. Our upbringing, family, educational, social, racial, linguistic, class and cultural background will have a significant bearing on our values and these, in turn, will influence how we respond to pressures. Our values and expectations will influence whether the coping strategy we choose increases, decreases or has no impact on the level of pressure encountered (Lazarus and Folkman, 1986).

Cherniss (1980) also argues that differences of value and theoretical orientation can be a source of tension between staff, possibly acting as a barrier to colleague support. And, in an earlier study (Cherniss *et al.*, 1979), he found that newer, more idealistic workers tended to avoid contact with their more experienced colleagues as they perceived them as cynical and lacking in dedication. Value conflict can therefore be seen to get in the way of effective teamwork.

Personality theory and the social worker

Social work staff are, simply by virtue of their occupation, likely to be exposed to a variety of pressures, some of them very significant. However, are there any personality factors that will influence how these pressures are experienced and dealt with? Pines and Kafry (1978) argue that social workers are a rather 'homogeneous group, emotionally whose sensitivity to clients' problems make them more vulnerable to stress' (p. 500). Similarly, Kadushin (1974) views social workers as people who are responsive to a 'dedicatory' ethic; that is, they view their work as a calling, and reward is considered to be inherent in the act of giving (p. 706). Identity and self-esteem can therefore be seen to interrelate with occupational role and performance.

Of course, we can surmise that the degree of homogeneity found within the social work profession is a result of the type of people who apply to become social workers and the screening devices used to select those with particular kinds of personality traits. In this way, the very attributes that motivate some people to become social workers may also be those that can make them more sensitive to the emotional pressures of the job (Pines and Kafry, 1978). It is therefore important that we do not discount the importance of personality, both in terms of stress resistance and from the perspective of service delivery.

Personality and coping

The effects of pressure and stress upon us will be governed by not only our personality and other individual differences, but also the coping strategies we use in an attempt to deal with them. Lazarus and Folkman (1986) define coping as the: 'person's constantly changing cognitive and behavioural efforts to meet specific external and/or internal demands that are appraised as taxing or exceeding a person's resources' (p. 141).

Hobfall (1988) comments that: 'coping strategies are likely to be maintained by a complex person–environment interaction; that is they are created and sustained because they meet individual needs in a given environment' (p. 300). Thus, it is up to each of us to choose the most positive methods that best suit our needs.

The multitude of coping strategies can be categorised under three general headings – those that:

1. Deal with the problem directly.
2. Re-evaluate the problem.
3. Accept the problem but minimise its effects.

Tubesing and Tubesing (1982) note how every individual: 'has a wealth of stress management strategies at his or her disposal. These skills have been learned and practised over a lifetime' (p. 160). However, the effectiveness of such strategies will vary according to a number of factors, such as personality, levels of support, socialisation and previous experience of dealing with similar situations. There is no simple or straightforward answer to the question of what makes for effective coping. However, as we have noted, there are two key guiding principles that we need to bear in mind with regard to coping:

1. We need to have a broad repertoire of coping methods in order to avoid the danger of 'putting all our eggs in one basket'.
2. It is important that we distinguish between constructive and destructive coping methods. For example, having a stiff drink may well be a constructive and appropriate response to pressure at times but heavy drinking runs the risk of becoming an even bigger problem (and therefore a further set of pressures) than the initial stressor.

Coping also needs to be seen in a wider context than just the characteristics of the individual. As Wiener (1989) notes, within social services people usually work in teams and: 'just as individuals react to stress in different ways so do teams' (p. 20). He goes on to comment that those who are popular, or have good interpersonal skills, are likely to find obtaining social support an easier task than those who may antagonise others or who find it difficult to express their emotions. The development of interpersonal skills can therefore be seen as a major method of avoiding stress or reducing its effects.

Practice Focus 3.3

This team of social workers were part of a small voluntary organisation, funded mainly by the host local authority. Suddenly, as a result of financial cutbacks, their grant was removed completely and they had to re-think, re-evaluate and reorganise their whole approach to the work. They had to generate income and had to live 'from hand to mouth', one month to the next.

In spite of these powerful stressors, the team became very cohesive and supportive. Team members commented that they had never felt so 'together' or so creative as a team. They were getting more, not less, satisfaction from the work that they were doing. In this way, the team collectively increased their ability to cope with the major pressure of massive organisational change.

Compare this with the team studied by Murphy (1991) who, although also under immense pressure, felt cut off and unable to support each other. One member described the feeling as like being in a bell-jar: 'I knew that everyone else was suffering; I could see the effects of stress on their behaviour, but I couldn't reach out to them – it was like being in a bell-jar.'

Wiener (1989) also highlights a number of informal rules that may exist within teams – rules that will tend to make asking for social support difficult. Amongst these he includes the 'wimp rule':

you can only ask for support when you admit you cannot do something – that is, you always ask someone to do a joint visit if you are really sure that you cannot cope. Another version of this rule happens in single cover residential work when a member of staff is told 'you can always phone me – if you are really in trouble'; in other words if you actually phone it's a sign that you are not up to the job (pp. 20–1).

A similar rule is what Wiener calls the 'macho' rule:

> this is a tough area/home/centre and before you have the right to ask for help you have to show that you can cope: you have to be tough to work here and if you are tough, you don't need support or, to put it another way, you can only ask for help if you do not need it (ibid., p. 21).

This emphasis on a masculine 'be tough' attitude is an important issue and one we shall return to later.

Personal coping strategies

There are many strategies that can be used to deal with the pressures we face. Some of these are outlined here, although we need to recognise that these represent only a small sample of the wide range available to us. This very important notion of coping with pressure and stress is also a topic we shall consider in more detail in Chapter 7.

Planning and goal-setting

One of the most popular stress management techniques is the development of what Newman and Beehr (1979) call 'personal planning skills'. They comment that: 'the individual who thinks about forthcoming events and the potential stress that may arise is seemingly in a better position to make a protective adaptive response' (p. 7). Planning is a way of ensuring that time and energy are used in the most efficient and effective manner possible. Personal planning is part of developing a systematic approach with clear objectives and a positive and proactive outlook. Planning therefore helps to increase our sense of control and, consequently, acts as a good safeguard against anxiety and a boost to confidence.

Re-evaluation

Often it is not possible to remove certain stressors and so our strategy for dealing with them may be to 're-evaluate' them, that is, to see them in a different light. For example, having to travel a long distance to a meeting may be a stressor that cannot be avoided but, if the travelling time is seen as 'thinking time' to prepare for the meeting, the effects of the pressure can be reduced.

Taylor (1983) argues that re-evaluation strategies have three primary goals:

1. To find meaning in experience;
2. To regain control over the event and one's life;
3. To restore self-esteem.

These are highly compatible with the approach we have adopted in this book in so far as they relate to: the importance of the subjective, as well as, objective dimension; the major contribution control can make, and the significant role of self-esteem. An example of a re-evaluation strategy can be found in research carried out by Schutz and Decker (1975). They found, in a sample of 100 people with spinal-cord injuries, that two-thirds reported they felt the disability had some positive consequences, such as becoming a better person and having a higher level of self-awareness.

Social comparison is another popular method of re-evaluating an event – the 'it could have been worse' mode of thinking. Taylor (1983), in a study of women with breast cancer found that those who coped most successfully compared themselves to others who were less fortunate than themselves. As Taylor puts it: 'in the final analysis everyone is better off than someone as long as one picks the right dimension' (quoted in Wade and Tavris, 1990, p. 550). However, in some situations, the use of social comparisons may prove counterproductive, as we may achieve less by lowering our standards or expectations through inappropriate comparisons with others. That is, we may set our sights too low by comparing ourselves with others who are less able, or less well-placed, to achieve what we are capable of.

Another commonly-used method of re-evaluation is that of humour. Humour has been shown to act as a buffer between stress and negative moods (Martin and Lefcourt, 1983). They found that a person's attitude towards a situation was significant. For example, people who were able to transform 'terrible news' into a sense of the absurd or illogical were found to be less prone to depression, anger, tension and fatigue than those who 'give in' to gloom. Rickford (1992) gives the example of one social worker who, when asked how she and her colleagues coped with intervening in people's lives, responded: 'We used humour – cracking jokes about clients – as a way of surviving. Most of the time they were harmless, but they could be quite hostile' (p. 14).

It is important to note, however, that humour should be seen as an appropriate coping strategy within certain boundaries. Humour can be of benefit in the form of venting feelings, without feeling exposed and vulnerable. In some situations, humour is used in a bid to detach ourselves from the pain or hopelessness of the situation we are in. However, in the final analysis, it is important that individuals remain in touch with the reality of their feelings, no matter how painful. A sense of balance or proportion needs to be achieved so that the positive value of humour does not become converted into a destructive force. For example, it has been suggested by Bramhall and Ezell (1981) that:

- becoming callous and cynical
- making 'sick' jokes
- ridiculing clients

are a manifestation of extreme stress and burnout.

We therefore need to be wary of the development of seemingly harmless humour, and be clear as to whether it is serving a positive or negative function. This is also significant in terms of the use of humour in depersonalising service users and sustaining and reinforcing discriminatory or oppressive stereotypes (Thompson, 1993). We shall return to this point in our discussions, in the Chapter 4, of the relationship between stress and such factors as racism and sexism. Humour therefore needs to be used selectively and sensitively.

Other strategies

The development of assertiveness skills has been recognised as an important coping strategy (see, for example, Girdano *et al.*, 1990) in so far as the ability to say 'no' and be clear about personal boundaries can play a major role in keeping pressures within manageable limits. (These are points to which we shall return in Chapter 7.) Rees and Graham (1991) describe assertiveness in the following terms:

> Being assertive is essentially about respecting yourself and others. It is about having a basic belief that your opinions, beliefs, thoughts and feelings are as important as anyone else's – and that this goes for other people too. It is about being in touch with your own needs and wants, but contrary to some misconceptions about assertive behaviour, it is not about going for what you want at any cost. To be assertive is to be able to express yourself clearly, directly and appropriately, to value what you think and feel, to have esteem and respect for yourself; to recognise your own strengths and limitations. In other words, to appreciate yourself for who you are. With this as a basis, it is then possible to learn specific techniques which will enable you to change your behaviour in the areas which you choose (p. 1).

'Changing your behaviour' can, of course, include stress-management behaviour – handling pressure and avoiding stress.

Dealing with stress is, though, not just about our own approach to life and work but also about the environment in which we operate. A useful coping strategy, therefore, is to seek to influence that environment as far as possible. This can include making the work environment more pleasant or more conducive to achieving job satisfaction. It could even mean changing the work environment altogether, for example, by changing jobs or trying to arrange a temporary transfer. But, even without having to take such relatively drastic steps, positive changes to the work environment can be made if people decide to do so. A useful first step in this direction is to include discussion of the environment on the agenda for a team or staff meeting.

Another useful aspect of coping is self-awareness, particularly awareness of the strengths we can draw on if called upon to do so. For example, Toffler (1970) makes reference to how important it is for people to be aware of their personal anchor points or 'stability zones', in order to provide a stable basis. As we saw in Chapter 2, these 'zones' include: relationships, activities, possessions and even organisations. A system of values is also an important stability zone for us: 'adherence to a particular system of principles for the conduct of one's life provides a stabilising, calming, composure that helps the individual handle the stresses of life' (Newman and Beehr, 1979, p. 8). The basic premise of this approach is that successful stress management is based on gaining an understanding of self and how we relate to others. That is, self-awareness has a significant bearing on interpersonal relationships and the sources of both pressure and support that derive from these. This view is also supported by Sutherland and Cooper (1991) who comment that: 'it is our firm belief that any success in dealing with stress must begin with self knowledge' (p. 226).

Continuing the theme of self-awareness, supportive self-talk is thought to be a critical factor in determining how we feel (Satir, 1975). We frequently find ourselves engaged in a 'self-dialogue' in which we shape how we should behave and feel about ourselves. Self-dialogue can be positive or negative. Negative self-dialogue is destructive and exacerbates the harmful effects of stress. It is therefore important for us to guard against unwittingly creating unnecessary additional pressures by adopting a negative attitude towards ourselves. Positive self-dialogue, by contrast, tends to have the effect of boosting self-esteem and helps to provide us with the confidence and personal resources to cope with pressure and fend off stress. Schwartz and Garamoni (1986) have argued that, in psychologically healthy individuals, the balance between positive and negative self thoughts is around 62 per cent positive cognitions to 38 per cent negative. Greater proportions of negative thoughts are associated with emotional disorder and psychological dysfunction.

Stress inoculation

Meichenbaum (1975) developed an approach based on the process of 'inoculating' ourselves against using or developing inappropriate coping strategies. By analogy with the medical process of immunisation against disease, we experience a small 'dose' of the potentially stressful situation in order to be able to counteract it in real life situations. Stress inoculation programmes usually involve the identification of the sources of stress, possibly by the use of role-play. Participants are then able to explore alternative strategies to deal with the situation, which they rehearse and test out in the real world. 'Inoculating' ourselves against stress is therefore a potentially very helpful approach to coping.

Fitness, health and diet

Coping skills aimed at enhancing an individual's physical well-being represent the more traditional approach to stress management (Tubesing and Tubesing, 1982). Exercise is seen as beneficial as it increases self-esteem, facilitates sleep, and aids the development of a healthier body. It can also be seen to be related to the ability to make and maintain interpersonal relationships which, as we have seen, is an integral part of coping with pressure and avoiding stress. Exercise has been well documented as contributing to the attainment and maintenance of physiological and psychological vitality, both important aspects of coping with pressure. In particular, aerobic exercise such as jogging, brisk walking, aerobic dancing and swimming have been highlighted as 'stress antidotes' (Sutherland and Cooper, 1991).

  Given the pressures of media and fashion to conform to the 'ideal body', plus the perceived relative extra costs of healthy eating, it may be seen as difficult to maintain a healthy diet. Nonetheless, the efforts needed to achieve success in this area are well repaid in terms of health, self-esteem and resistance to stress, especially if our attempts to achieve a good diet are not unrealistic and overly ambitious in the initial stages. If the changes in our eating habits and lifestyle are to become established and long-term, then we need to ensure that we adjust carefully and steadily without falling into the trap of trying to achieve too much too soon, thereby guaranteeing that we fail and lose our motivation to try again.

Relaxation is another health-related approach to coping with stress. There are many ways to relax, but what may be relaxing for one person may be a chore for another (for example, gardening). There are numerous relaxation training techniques such as controlled breathing, yoga, meditation, and so on. The majority of these techniques rely on a body–mind connection and a process of mentally letting go of our stress.

Also, a limited degree of self-indulgence in the form of 'treating' ourselves can help us appreciate the energy we have spent in overcoming a stressful task and can therefore be a much needed boost to self-esteem at times when pressures and demands upon us are at a high level. However, this clearly has financial implications and is therefore a relevant aspect of the social context in which pressure, stress and coping occur – the subject matter of Chapter 4.

Conclusion

In order to deal effectively with stress and pressure we need to have a clear grasp of the various key elements of this complex area of study. The relationship between stress and the individual is one such key element. This chapter has therefore sought to throw some light on the ways in which personality factors interact with issues of pressure and stress.

This has been tackled at two levels. First, we explored some of the many theoretical approaches to the study of personality and considered what implications these had for our understanding of the phenomena of pressure and stress. Second, we examined a range of coping methods commonly used to good effect in dealing with stress. It is to be hoped that the discussions here will help social work staff to achieve a better understanding of stress and how their personality interacts with it. Furthermore, it is hoped that this greater understanding can be instrumental in leading to an enhanced level of coping; that is, the aim is a practical one. The theory and research base outlined here is not an end in itself. Rather, it is presented as a means to the practical end of helping social work staff become better equipped to deal with the pressures they inevitably face.

However, being better equipped to deal with stress does not depend only on personal, individual matters. It also hinges on a range of social and organisational factors. The social factors form the subject matter of Chapter 4 whilst organisational factors are discussed in Chapters 5 and 6. It will be helpful, therefore, if the personal dimension of stress explored here can be seen in its broader social and organisational context. The points made and issues raised in Chapters 4–6 should therefore be seen as a continuation and development of the ideas presented here rather than as an alternative to them. Stress is a phenomenon which is simultaneously personal *and* social *and* organisational. All three dimensions have a significant part to play and so we should be wary of making the common mistake of looking upon stress in too narrow a focus.

4

The Social Context

Understanding individual and personality factors in relation to pressure and stress is an important element in the development of a theory base to underpin the practice of stress management. However, what we must also realise is that such factors operate in a social context. This can be seen to apply in a number of ways:

- individual identity has social roots; that is, our sense of self is heavily dependent on our 'social location' – where we fit into society, the cultural expectations to which we have been exposed, and so on
- individuals are members of groups and so questions of group dynamics, intergroup conflict and so on are very relevant
- the coping resources and support systems to which we have access will be structured according to our social position (for example, buying power)
- oppression and discrimination arising from structured inequalities act as significant stressors for certain groups within the workforce

These represent a broad range of social factors that impinge on, constrain, condition and shape personality or identity. As Berger (1966) puts it:

What happens in socialization is that the social world is internalized within the child. The same process, though

69

perhaps weaker in quality, occurs every time the adult is initiated into a new social context or a new social group. Society, then, is not only something 'out there' in the Durkheimian sense, but is also 'in here', part of our innermost being (p. 140).

The sociological basis of stress is a vast subject and certainly one which cannot be covered adequately within a single chapter. For this reason our focus here is much narrower and concentrates on the specific area of 'social divisions', a term used to describe the social categories of class, race, gender and so on which 'form the basis of the social structure – the "network" of social relationships, institutions and groupings – which plays such an important role in the distribution of power, status and opportunities' (Thompson, 1993, p. 15). But even this is too broad a field to tackle in the space available to us. We shall therefore limit ourselves to discussion of two of these divisions, those of race and gender. We have chosen these two specific areas, partly because of their major links with issues of pressure and stress, and partly because of their significance with regard to developing anti-oppressive practice. We shall begin by considering how issues of race and ethnicity have a significant impact on the complex matter of pressure and stress in social work.

Race, oppression and stress

McDerment (1992) argues that: 'Women managers constitute the major target group for stress related diseases, and people from black and ethnic minority groups are particularly vulnerable to dysfunctional stress' (p. 13). This view, in relation to black workers, is also supported by an empirical study undertaken in the London Borough of Brent. Wilkinson and Wilson (1992) comment:

The stress of being a black worker in a predominantly white setting has been high-lighted in a recent study which examined staff stress and satisfaction in a community psychogeriatric service. It found that average stress ratings among black staff in direct care provision were *twice* as high as those for white staff in the areas of client aggression, assumption of tasks of a family member, inability of a carer to let go of a client, and in working with people in the last stage of life. In nearly all other situations, though the difference was not as marked, black staff on average, recorded higher stress ratings (p. 16).

The picture this is beginning to paint is one of an occupation which is recognised as being a highly pressurised one – and yet it appears to be even more pressurised for black or ethnic minority staff. At one level, this is hardly surprising, given what we know about the effects of racism in modern society. Since the mid-1980s social work has become increasingly aware of the existence and significance of racism not only within wider society but also within social work itself.

Hugman (1991) comments on the obstacles that black people can experience in attempting to gain entry to the caring professions. In many cases overt racism can be seen to be operating. However, he points out that this is not necessarily the result of personal prejudice or racism at an individual level. Rather, he sees it as an example of institutional racism:

Institutional racism differs from personal racism in that it arises not from conscious acts but from the failure of practitioners, managers and policy makers to recognise the power structures of the everyday world in which power is exercised by white people without their awareness. The consequence is seen in statements that 'this organisation is not racist' or that 'we treat everyone the same' which are not disingenuous, but which fail to take account of the differential distribution of social power. This analysis follows from the understanding of white racism not simply as a set of personal practices on the part of deviant individuals, but as part of the fabric of society (p. 149).

This raises a number of significant issues with regard to the relationship between racism, on the one hand, and pressure and stress on the other. These include:

- black staff will experience racism even in the absence of overt acts of prejudice
- racism has insidious and subtle effects which may not be immediately recognisable
- if agencies and staff do not adopt a positive and explicit strategy of anti-racism, they will be reinforcing and/or condoning racism; there is no neutral middle ground — we are either part of the solution or part of the problem (Thompson, 1993)
- racism is measured in terms of its discriminatory and oppressive *effects*, rather than intentions

This important concept of *institutional* racism is one to which we shall return later. But first, there are other aspects of racism that merit our attention.

Practice Focus 4.1

Mohamed was in his mid-twenties. After a period of time as a youth worker, he became a residential social worker at a children's centre. He was a Muslim but not strict in his religious observances. He did not see himself as, in any sense 'radical', nor particularly knowledgeable about issues of race and racism.

From his first day he felt quite uncomfortable. It was not that any member of staff was particularly hostile to him but, rather, a mixture of the following issues:

1. He suspected that other staff felt he had only got the job because he was black.
2. The only other black member of staff to work at the centre had left some months previously but a veil of secrecy surrounded why she had left.
3. A number of jokes, especially those told by the male members of staff were vaguely racist in tone and content.
4. He became aware that little consideration was given to the needs of children from other ethnic groups;

when he raised this issue, the responses he received
included:

'We have no black children here – it isn't a
problem.'

'If ever we do get any black children here we will
treat them the same as anyone else.'

Now that we've got you, everything will be all
right.'

These comments made Mohamed feel very uncomfortable. He felt that he was seen to be 'rocking
the boat' and was beginning to be labelled as a
trouble-maker.

A major expectation in social work practice is that, as far as
possible, a positive rapport be established between worker and
client. This is often difficult, especially in social control
situations as, for example, in many child protection cases.
However, for black workers, there are additional pressures to
face, arising partly from racism on the part of clients, and
partly from poorly thought out attempts, on the part of some
agencies, to develop a multicultural practice. Let us look at
each of these two aspects in turn.

First, black workers will often be subject to overt and direct
racism on the part of white clients. To be rejected, ridiculed,
and generally devalued by service users understandably
comprises a major stressor in its own right. However, when
the expectation is that social work staff will adopt an attitude
of 'unconditional positive regard', this amounts to something
of a tall order when black staff are confronted by racial abuse
or other forms of personal racism.

In describing the racial killing of an Asian schoolboy by a
white pupil, Gus John (1991) comments that the aggressor was
as much a victim of British racism as the child killed. This
illustrates the view of racism as an oppressive ideology and set
of social practices into which we are all socialised. This means
that racist behaviour towards black staff will not be
uncommon as such incidents reflect dominant and pervasive
assumptions of white superiority. But, of course, these

assumptions are not free-floating or the result of an unhappy coincidence – they are inextricably linked to the structural basis of society, to issues of class and economic exploitation (Williams, 1989; Ramdin, 1987).

The implication of this analysis is that racial abuse by white clients is often not only a *form* of oppression (for black workers) but also partly a *result* of oppression, a class-based oppression arising from the 'divide and conquer' tactic which sets white against black within the working class:

> There are close links between race and class. Indeed, racism can be seen as an ideology which divides the working class by setting worker against worker and thereby contributes to the continuance of capitalism by discouraging working-class solidarity (Hall, 1980). However, it is a mistake to see the social division of race as a sub-category of class. Class and race articulate together; that is, they are inter-related (Thompson, 1993, p. 75).

These are complex issues beyond the scope of this text. The point remains, however, that a black worker exposed to racism from a client faces a far more difficult and complex situation than other racist experiences. Racism is, therefore, not only a life pressure at a general level, but also a specific occupational stressor as a result of the role ambiguity and dilemmas inherent in such situations. What often makes such incidents even more potentially stressful is the lack of support from white colleagues. As Peter Ferns (1987) comments: 'In my past experience as a black manager supervising white staff, I have often felt isolated and unsupported, especially when dealing with overtly racist staff and clients' (p. 19).

Practice Focus 4.2

Almost two years after Mohamed took up post (see Practice Focus 4.1), the centre admitted its first black resident in several years. Daniel was a fourteen year old boy with an Irish mother and a Ghanaian father. Daniel regarded himself as white and made it clear he wanted to be seen as such at the centre.

Mohamed felt the pressures increasing. Instead of trying to find out what Daniel's background meant to him, Mohamed's colleagues seemed to be implying: 'See, we told you it wouldn't be a problem.' Consequently, Mohamed felt confused, alienated and isolated from the staff group, and began to perceive his work environment as a very stressful one.

Hutchinson-Reis (1989) also comments on the lack of colleague support and even goes so far as to argue that the actions of colleagues often also have a racist impact:

> Black social workers are often assumed by their white colleagues to be newly qualified, off access courses or former nurses. In addition, black workers are often perceived as clients themselves or received with disbelief by other agencies. In general they do not receive the same consideration from colleagues and others and are not attributed with the same academic and professional status as whites. Black workers seldom receive the support of their white colleagues when confronting racist clients or others (p. 170).

A second set of factors that stack the odds against black workers derives from the mishandled attempts of some social work agencies to deal with issues of race and ethnicity. This tends to take two forms:

1. *Lumping*. This is where cultural differences between black workers and the clients or communities they serve are not taken into account. Peter Ferns (1987) comments:

> There seems to be a trend for black workers to be almost automatically allocated to black clients without any sensitivity to the needs of workers or clients. For instance, Asian clients are allocated to Asian workers regardless of which Asian culture they have. Black

workers can be useful to some black clients as they share a common experience of racism in this country; but there are times when this issue is not relevant to the primary needs of black clients (pp. 19–20).

This tendency to regard black people as a homogeneous group can create considerable tensions and conflicts for black social work staff. Again this acts as a source of additional pressure.

2. *Dumping*. This is where black staff are assumed to be experts in race relations. They are expected to take a lead in promoting ethnically-sensitive and anti-racist practice. As Dominelli (1989) puts it: '*Dumping strategies* rely on placing the responsibility for eliminating racism on black people's shoulders' (p. 394). Needless to say, this is yet another source of additional pressure for black workers.

The points raised here in relation to black workers can also be seen to apply to black students to the same, or even a greater extent. Several authors refer to the difficulties experienced by black students on social work qualifying courses (for example, Pink, 1991; de Gale, 1991; de Souza, 1991). Some of the themes which emerge are:

• tokenism and mere lip-service to issues of anti-racism
• the lack of a systematic approach to anti-discriminatory practice
• a higher than average failure rate for black students due, in part, to a lack of support mechanisms
• a shortage of black practice teachers or practice teachers skilled and experienced in anti-racist practice
• a devaluing of black experience and expertise

Clearly there is a need for black students to receive a better service so that (a) they do not have to contend with unnecessary additional pressures and (b) they can receive the support they need and deserve. A social work education system which promotes empowerment and yet disempowers its black students is a system that contributes more to stress than to stress management.

As far as coping methods are concerned, issues of ethnicity and racism are also relevant, although once again, this is from a negative point of view. In our earlier discussions of coping resources, we identified a number of important contributory factors to positive coping. Two key elements amongst these were control and a positive approach based on high self-esteem, and yet these can both be seen to be undermined by the negative effects of racism. Institutional racism can leave black staff feeling they have little control over their work or career plans – they are disempowered. They can feel powerless in a white-dominated organisation which pays little or no attention to the needs of black clients or workers. Similarly, the negative images of black people inherent in racism can undermine positive self images and self-esteem. As Webb and Tossell (1991) comment:

> The influence of racism is felt at a very early age. Young children are aware of the differences in themselves and other children and soon recognize which colour is more highly valued by society. There have been examples of young black children scrubbing themselves 'in order to become white'. This point was made by the CRE who state in *From Cradle to School* (1989), 'We know from research evidence that by the time they enter primary school, white children may well be on the way to believing they are superior to black people. Black children may believe that society is not going to show them the same respect and esteem that white people receive' (p. 81).

Ideally, social work agencies should support and value their black staff to such an extent that they can overcome any such demeaning early life experiences and develop a positive professional self-image. However, as we have seen, the literature paints a very different picture. The detrimental effects of racism in the wider society can be seen to be echoed and reinforced within social work – rather than confronted and challenged. This does not mean that all black workers have low self-esteem, but rather that self-esteem can be far more difficult to achieve, much more of an uphill struggle. In short, racism can undermine coping resources and leave black staff more vulnerable to stress. This emphasises the need for a positive black identity to be fostered and for the role and contribution of black staff to be appreciated:

> The position of black workers employed in predominantly white organisations needs to be recognised. Anti-racism must be a humanitarian endeavour in which black and white workers can work together to combat the oppression that black people, clients and colleagues, experience. Unless and until a supportive environment is created for black workers, the number of black workers will remain low (Thompson, 1993, p. 80).

As we shall emphasise in Chapter 6, managers have a responsibility to play a supportive role with regard to helping staff operate within the optimal pressure range without this overspilling into stress. As far as black staff are concerned, this responsibility is even greater for managers as it entails recognising, and dealing with, the additional stressors encountered and the barriers to coping resources and support. Clearly, there is more to understanding stress and stress management than an analysis of personality factors or the personal circumstances of the individual; social factors such as ethnicity and racism also have a key role to play if our grasp of the vitally important topic of stress management is to be anything other than superficial. In view of this, we now need to broaden our analysis further and begin to take on board issues of gender, as these too have major implications for the management of pressure and stress.

Gender and stress

It is important to recognise, right at the start, that the majority of social work and social care practitioners are women, whereas the majority of managers are men:

> Women are the main users and providers of social services but they have little say in how these services are organised or managed. Whilst eighty-six percent of all staff working

in social services departments are women, seventy-nine percent of their senior managers are men (SSI, 1992, p. 1).

Increasingly it is being recognised that organisations tend to be shaped by male values and perspectives (Lupton, 1992). This can result in the majority of the workforce (that is, women) finding it difficult to have their needs and abilities recognised, and finding aspects of the organisation's conduct increasing their pressures. Clear examples of this would be the reluctance of most social work agencies to recognise the importance in achieving promotion above the level of team leader. In a small-scale study undertaken by McDerment (1988) one of the factors she identified was: 'The male domination of the organization which led to sexism in appointments and in dealing with women's issues. This was confirmed by the number of women who reported a feeling of frustration because their wish for promotion seemed blocked' (p. 77).

Morgan (1986) also offers apt comment:

Many organizations are dominated by gender-related values that bias organizational life in favour of one sex over another. Thus organizations often segment opportunity structures and job markets in way that enable men to achieve positions of prestige and power more easily than women, and often operate in ways that produce gender-related biases in the way organizational reality is created and sustained on a day-to-day basis. This is most obvious in situations of open discrimination and various forms of sexual harassment, but often pervades the culture of an organization in a way that is much less visible (p. 178, quoted in Mills and Murgatroyd, 1991, p. 68).

We shall return to the question of sexual harassment below but, first, there are two other points arising from this passage that merit further discussion:

1. There is a parallel here with the experience of black workers in predominantly white organisations. That is, female staff have to face the pressures of working in a

male-dominated context where their interests generally take second place. Consequently, women have less access to power, greater barriers to job satisfaction and to career progression. In short, female staff are subject to institutional sexism.

2. The dominance of a male perspective tends to reinforce a 'be tough' culture which can deter both female and male workers from seeking help in dealing with stress (Murphy, 1991; see also Chapter 7 below). Male dominance can be seen to contribute to an ethos or culture in which expression of feeling is discouraged and talk of pressure and stress is seen as a sign of weakness. Male dominance therefore acts as a barrier to effective stress management.

Such a masculine-biased organisational culture also creates an atmosphere in which sexist actions and attitudes are more likely to go unchallenged and be tolerated or even encouraged. This means that female staff are vulnerable to sexist discrimination and oppression not only from clients but also from colleagues. Let us consider, in turn, each of these two sources of oppression, and thus of pressure and stress.

Women in social work frequently come up against both overt and more subtle forms of sexism in their dealings with service users. For example, where a male and female undertake joint work, it will often be assumed that the male worker is the more senior of the two. Also, female social work staff will often be patronised or have their professionalism undermined or challenged. At times, they may even be subject to direct sexual harassment or seen as a legitimate sexual 'target'.

Practice Focus 4.3

Val was a specialist child protection worker. She was allocated the case of the Dempsey family. Mr Dempsey's two grown up daughters had accused him of sexually abusing them many years earlier when they were young children. He had been arrested but no prosecution had been brought due to a lack of evidence. He had now remarried and become step-father to two girls, aged nine and eight. As a result of the previous allegations, the girls' names were placed on the child protection register.

Val visited the family home to introduce herself and explain the nature of her involvement. When she told Mr Dempsey she wished to visit on a regular basis, he commented: 'Anyone with a pretty face like yours can visit me anytime they like.' Val was very annoyed by this comment and the blatant attempt to use sexism to undermine her professional role. However, she handled the situation very well by responding assertively: 'As you very well know, what I look like is not the issue; we need to be clear about the reasons for my visits.'

Sadly, sexism is not confined to dealings with clients. It can, and does, arise from within our own work settings and in our interactions with other agencies. In addition to the institutional sexism which produces a noticeable imbalance in the distribution of power in social work agencies (Howe, 1986a), women staff are also susceptible to more direct and visible experiences of sexism. Fogarty (1987), reporting on interviews with a number of female social workers, comments that:

Their experiences of overt and covert sexism will put paid to any smug notion that male social workers are less sexist than your average wolf whistling building site worker. The comments and gestures may – only may – be less crude, but if the experiences of these randomly chosen women are anything to go by, forget the namby pamby liberal stuff. Female social workers have still got one hell of an uphill struggle to change attitudes (pp. 13–14).

Practice Focus 4.4

Cathy was an experienced social worker in a mental health team. She enjoyed her work, particularly the more challenging aspects of it. However, when Tom took over as the new team leader, she noticed a significant change in her workload. She realised that the tasks allocated to her tended to be much more routine and undemanding than she had been used to. She didn't comment on this at first but, after a period of time, she became increasingly restless and dissatisfied. She therefore felt she had to raise this with Tom, and subsequently did so in a supervision session. She was both infuriated and disgusted by his response when he commented that he didn't believe in exposing women to potentially dangerous situations. This, he claimed, was a job more suited to the male members of the team while the female members had more to offer through nurturing the less demanding clients. Cathy was speechless and wondered whether she would be able to continue to work with this man.

These issues can be particularly significant for women managers in social work. The sexism they encounter highlights what Hanmer and Statham (1988) describe as the 'double jeopardy' of being a female manager, the challenge of succeeding in a male-dominated world without reinforcing, or becoming part of, the masculine ethos. And, as Cooper and Davidson (1982) point out, this becomes an additional stressor for them. Allan *et al.* (1992) also recognise the difficulties and pressures for women managers within male-dominated Social Services Departments:

Male networks and clubs and communication patterns, offer men information sharing and decision making outside the formal organisational culture. Women, excluded from this, feel their effectiveness undermined. Certain sections of departments are viewed as well defended male preserves. Women managers therefore face additional stresses. The organisational culture offers little recognition of balancing family and work responsibilities. It seems to give lower value to women's contribution, therefore requiring them to do better to succeed equally. Being in a minority because of gender and race means that many women managers feel their contributions are marginalised while their mistakes are all too visible (p. 3).

This is another example of the detrimental effects of institutional sexism on women, in this case women managers. The additional stressors can be seen to be of major proportions.

Also of major significance for women staff is the continued existence of sexual harassment at work. This is a topic which is frequently the target for a great deal of (inappropriate) humour. It is a very serious matter with huge implications in terms of the management of pressure and stress. The report of the Department of Health Social Services Inspectorate (SSI, 1991) describes sexual harassment in the following terms: 'Unwelcome sexual comments, looks, actions, suggestions or physical contact can cause great distress to women and damage confidence, job performance and promotion prospects' (p. 53).

Hopkins (1987b) describes an American study of 319 social workers with regard to sexual harassment:

The survey showed that social workers were victimised by co-workers and clients as well as by supervisors and administrators. Over one third of the women and one seventh of the men surveyed had experienced such victimisation. The most frequent kind of approach was verbal harassment in the form of sexually oriented jokes, propositions and demeaning flattery. But some victims had experienced unwanted touching, fondling and kissing (p. 13).

Sexual harassment is a clear reflection of gender oppression within an organisation. The pressures generated by such incidents can, in themselves, be immense. However, what can prove to be an even greater stressor is the organisational response to such situations. In some cases the situation is trivialised or seen as 'just a joke', or an over-reaction by an over-sensitive woman. In other cases, the recourse to formal procedures can lead to considerable tension and ill-feeling. As the SSI report puts it: 'The process of pursuing sexual harassment complaints through formal procedures is always very distressing for the woman concerned' (SSI, 1991, p. 53).

Practice Focus 4.5

Sheila was a young but quite experienced fieldworker. She was confident in her ability as a practitioner, and quite assertive in her dealings with colleagues and managers. On joining a new team Sheila found herself the victim of increasingly oppressive sexual harassment by her manager.

After several blunt rejections of his behaviour, Sheila found that the problem became worse instead of better. Having made an official complaint and insisting on moving teams, Sheila became increasingly exasperated by the organisation's inability to deal with the situation satisfactorily. Several months later, Sheila left the agency; the manager remained. On review, Sheila stated that the stress due to the harassment itself had been very strong, but that the way the organisation had failed to deal with the harassment had, in fact, proven to be even more stressful.

It is clear that, if the organisation does not control and appropriately deal with, abuse or harassment, the practitioner concerned can feel herself to be doubly stressed. It is therefore important for social work agencies to develop staff care policies which include, at the very least, sensitive and supportive means of dealing with cases of sexual harassment. However, what is really needed is: 'a culture and climate within which women are valued and where these procedures are no longer required' (SSI, 1991, p. 53).

Women within social work agencies can clearly be seen to be subject to a number of additional stressors. However, there are also significant impediments to coping for female staff.

Perhaps the most major of these is the prevalence of the belief that women are 'natural' copers, that they are naturally more resistant to stress. This is a reflection of patriarchal ideology which casts women in the role of carers, and extension of the role of mother. As New and David (1985) put it:

> Women are given caring work on the grounds that they are mothers, or may become mothers. They are even expected to feel like mothers while they work as teachers, social workers, nurses or help out at the playgroup, and to be satisfied with no pay or low pay (p. 13).

Webb and Tossell (1991) also argue that social work agencies have tended to exploit women's propensity to act as carers by not supporting them in circumstances where they are more likely to support men. Lawrence (1992) argues that women are not encouraged to express negative emotions. Ideologically, they are presented as people who provide care, rather than people who need care. She relates this to the way women are socialised into specific gender roles and expectations. She explains this in the following terms:

> Under patriarchy, it is the task of the mother to induct her daughter into the role of second-class citizen. She may not do this in overt ways, but rather through the detail of the relationship she sets up. Like herself, her daughter must orientate herself towards meting the needs of others. She must learn from her mother to be a carer and not expect to be cared for in any but the most superficial sense. As a woman who has only partially had her own needs met, she encourages her daughter not to expect too much (p. 36).

Sexism constructs a situation in which women may feel guilty about having unmet needs, as they have been 'trained' to see the needs of others as having priority over their own. This has significant implications in terms of stress management for women:

- a prevailing ideology of women as natural copers will lead to many needs going unrecognised

- a focus on caring for others may result in a narrow repertoire of coping methods or self-care skills
- self-esteem can be adversely affected by the ethos of self-sacrifice promoted by patriarchy
- caring for others tends to promote an external, rather than internal, locus of control

All of these factors can be seen to act as barriers to effective coping, thus leaving women more susceptible to stress. And, because women are expected to cope, any signs of weakness or not bearing up are particularly noticeable – their significance is amplified. This presents a clear paradox: patriarchal ideology promotes an image of women as *resistant* to stress and yet it is precisely this ideology which, if anything, renders women *vulnerable* to stress. Lawrence (1992) shows how this applies to the way in which black women are perceived and treated:

> We have even created a racist stereotype of the black woman as someone who is able to cope with all kinds of hardship and emotional deprivation as though she had no feelings or needs at all. It is against this absurd and hostile stereotype that we tend to measure the actual capabilities of all black women (p. 38).

This clearly illustrates that the social context is so important if our attempts to understand the basis of stress are to be successful . A further aspect of this social context which relates to both gender and stress is that of the inter-relationship of home and work or, to put it more technically, the home–work interface. The importance of different 'spheres' has traditionally been given attention in the stress literature. It has long been recognised that extreme pressures in one sphere (for example, work) can be tolerated, provided that some degree of respite is offered in the other. (This relates closely to Toffler's concept of 'stability zones' discussed in Chapter 2.) However, what has not received full attention is the significance of gender with regard to the interaction of the two spheres of home and work.

For highly-paid professional workers, child care and other domestic support facilities can be bought to reduce the pressures of the 'double shift' – the situation so many working women encounter when they face the combined demands of paid work and unpaid domestic work at home. However, for many – if not most – women in social work, this type of paid help is not a possibility. Consequently, such women staff face what can be a very difficult balancing act between home and work responsibilities. Cooper and Davidson quote one woman who experiences such difficulties:

A potential source of stress which I've been able to keep at bay so far is at the end of the day having to deal with two children and playing fair by them and managing to switch modes, rather than putting my feet up and having a drink. I get little help from my husband (p. 144).

When this is combined with the view of women as 'natural copers' who need little or no support, we obtain a picture where:

- *pressures* are high, with each sphere offering little or no respite from the other
- little time or space for *coping methods* to be developed or utilised, for example, little or no leisure time
- a lack of *support* and little understanding of the need for support

Stress management for women who find themselves in such circumstances is no straight-forward matter. The aim of anti-discriminatory practice is to replace, as far as possible, oppression with empowerment. Clearly, this is something which must be seen to apply to women staff as well as women clients for, as Weinstein and Zappert (1985) put it: 'In attempting to integrate the often conflicting role demands of worker, spouse, and mother, women may be confronting stresses that pose serious hazards to their physical and psychological well-being' (p. 1174).

The linkages between stress and gender are, as we hope this section has shown, complex and intricate with a considerable amount of theorising and research yet to be done. Phillipson (1992) argues that: 'The management of stress is an example of an area where there may well be submerged gender dynamics: women frequently act as stress absorbers for others, particularly men' (p. 43). We would put it more strongly than this and contend that gender is a key dimension of the social context of the management of pressure and stress. As Phillipson's use of the term '*submerged* gender dynamics' suggests, gender is a key aspect of organisational culture.

Conclusion

Race and gender are good examples of the important part the social context must play in our understanding of the complex dynamics that underpin the experience of pressure and stress. As was emphasised at the beginning of this chapter, these are not the only social factors that have a part to play but are, rather, examples of a wide range of social factors and divisions that feature as strands in the intricate web of stress management.

Age, language, religion, disability and sexual orientation are further elements of the social context that have a bearing on what pressures are experienced and also on *how* they are experienced. The sociological basis of stress is one that has received far less attention than its psychological cousin and is therefore a relatively under-researched area. However, it is not even just a matter of understanding each of these different social factors. We also need to appreciate how these factors inter-relate and affect each other. For example, in this chapter we have focused on race and gender, yet we have said little about how the two factors intertwine. That is, issues of race and gender both apply to the experiences of black women in social work but it is not simply the case that they experience racism and sexism: 'Race does not simply make the experience of women's subordination greater, it qualitatively changes the nature of that subordination' (Langan, 1992, p. 5). We are only at the beginning of our understanding of how social factors interact with each other, and with pressure and stress.

The fact that we have so much to learn about such matters can, in itself, be seen as a significant stressor. For so long social work failed to take on board issues of discrimination and oppression and has only relatively recently begun to address the difficult questions raised. Developing anti-discriminatory practice, involves a certain amount of 'unlearning' what we have previously learned – challenging and undermining the discriminatory and oppressive attitudes and values into which we have previously been socialised. This can be a difficult and painful process, involving considerable discomfort and anxiety. Thus, genuine attempts to promote anti-discriminatory practice also generate additional pressures although, of course, this is no justification for giving up on such efforts. As this chapter has shown, women and black staff face additional pressures in social work without adequate support systems in place. The pressures involved in establishing an anti-oppressive ethos must therefore be recognised as a small price to pay for making a positive contribution to creating a less oppressive, and therefore less stressful, work environment.

This and the previous chapter have explored the personal and social dimensions of stress. Our next task is to examine the organisational dimension and this, indeed, is the subject matter of the next two chapters, Chapter 5 focusing on the specifics of the social work task and Chapter 6 addressing broader organisational issues.

5

The Social Work Task

This is the first of two chapters which address wider organisational aspects of social work stress. Chapter 6 explores those aspects that are largely related to the ways in which social work agencies are organised and managed – the factors that can be improved if the political will to bring about change exists or can be generated. The focus of this chapter, by contrast, is on those aspects of social work that cannot be changed – the factors that are intrinsic to the nature of the social work enterprise.

Social work carries with it a number of pressures and tensions which, although they may be reduced or mediated, will never disappear altogether – they are part and parcel of the fundamental basis of social work. A good example of this, and one we shall explore in more detail below, is the tension between care and control. This, together with many other such factors, is something we have to learn to live with if we are not to experience undue stress in our social work role.

One major implication of this is that a key element of successful stress management is to be able to recognise those factors that we cannot change or control. Having recognised them, we must then learn to adjust to them. This is recognised in the prayer which encourages us to work towards achieving the courage to work to change the things that can be changed, the strength to accept the things that cannot be changed, and the wisdom to know the difference between the two. It is with this aim in mind that we discuss a range of potential sources of stress that are simply not going to go away. If we are going to be able to fend off stress, then we need to consider strategies

90

for coping with these 'intrinsic stressors', to give them their formal title. This chapter aims to set the scene for doing just that.

The agency context

A point we have sought to emphasise in this text is that stress within social work should not be measured or conceived solely in terms of the individual practitioner. We need to see the pressure and stress experienced by the individual in the wider context; we should not 'blame the victim': 'Social work agencies need to remember just how stressful social work can be and, when an employee shows clear signs of stress, the question should not be: "What is the weakness in this employee?", but what is the weakness in the organisation that allows this to happen?' (Thompson, 1991a, p. viii).

The dangers involved in 'individualising' stress are now being increasingly recognised. There are signs that we are beginning to move away from a model of stress which locates the problem within the individual. This is illustrated by the following comment from a practitioner interviewed as part of a stress research study: 'The reason for the stress wasn't within me, it was in the task and the system. I wanted them to deal with those rather than look at my personal issues' (Murphy, 1991, p. 13).

Here is a social worker explaining her reasons for not accepting an offer of stress counselling after experiencing a period of exceptionally high pressure. For this worker, to have accepted that help would have amounted to admitting that the cause of stress was in herself, rather than in the wider context of the system in which she operated or the impossible demands of the task itself.

It is therefore important for us to develop a good understanding of those potentially stressful elements of the organisational context in which social work takes place. As we shall see in Chapter 6, many of these organisational stressors are avoidable and result from poor management practice and/ or problems arising from the agency's organisational culture or structure. However, many of the stressors are an inevitable part of social work and therefore pose a different challenge in terms of stress management. It is this latter group of pressure points which interests us here and so we shall now move on to consider some of the more major factors and how they impinge on social work personnel in their day to day work.

Dealing with people

Social work is, of course, primarily to do with people, rather than with the production or exchange of goods, wealth or knowledge. This has a number of important implications and so it is worth focusing, albeit briefly, on each of them in turn.

Uncertainty

The fact that social work is about the interactions between people means that its value to society is not easily measured. More importantly the 'raw material' of the social work task (that is, individual people, families and communities) are not predictable in a scientific or logical manner. Consequently, social work will inevitably be largely reactive, responding to unpredictable demands. Masson and Morrison (1991) echo the significant role of unpredictability and uncertainty, particularly in relation to duty work: 'The uncertainty of being on duty, the anxiety arising out of being unsure whether anything substantial is going to happen and being in a constant state of readiness in case it does, is one of the stresses associated with duty periods and referral and investigative work generally' (p. 366).

Echoing this theme, but specifically in relation to residential work, Dunham (1988) quotes from the report of one worker:

Insecurity is the cause of much stress amongst people I work with and it appears to be the result of the unpredictability of the behaviour of the residents. The staff rarely know what to expect next and this threatens their security by reducing their control over the environment. This insecurity is increased by direct confrontation with the residents (p. 57).

No amount of training, skill or experience will altogether remove the uncertainty inherent in social work, although there are, of course, ways in which it can be reduced, for example by planning and the appropriate application of research findings. The task, therefore, is twofold. On the one hand, steps to reduce uncertainty will also reduce the pressure and anxiety such uncertainty generates. On the other hand, we must learn to adapt to, and accommodate, those elements of uncertainty that cannot be eliminated (see Thompson, 1990, for a fuller discussion of uncertainty in social work).

Vulnerability, pain and suffering

The unpredictable demands referred to above, although a source of significant pressure in themselves, can give rise to an additional set of pressures and tensions in relation to the vulnerability of so many of the people who need to call upon social work help. As one of the social workers in Fineman's sample explained: 'I have really worried about the problems left over by Friday afternoon. It's worrying because it is people I'm dealing with, not goods standing in a half-finished state of manufacture. There's that awful stress from this' (1985, p. 66). Also, 'the severity of my clients' problems makes my job demanding' was identified as an important work pressure in the recent study of Hertfordshire social workers (Jones *et al.*, 1991).

Social workers are involved daily with individuals whose 'stress scores' are extremely high. Social workers can easily take on board much of this suffering and thereby experience a 'mirroring' in which their attempts to remain emotionally neutral are overpowered by the sheer intensity of feeling to which they are exposed. That is, empathy gives way to sympathy.

We also need to recognise that clients are apt to make considerable emotional demands on those working with them as a result of the stresses to which they are subject. For example, Gibson *et al.* (1989) report that, in their study, the emotional demands of clients caused moderate to high levels of stress in 48 per cent of their sample. Coming face to face with clients' emotions on such a regular basis can be a considerable source of pressure for the worker. And, of course, dealing constantly with the intense emotions of others means that we have to keep in touch with our own feelings. Attempting to do so places an extra demand upon us, but failing to do so will no doubt prove far more stressful in the long run. The 'feelings' dimension of our work is, of course, one that we ignore at our peril.

In terms of the mirroring of stress and dealing with pain and strong emotions, one of the best examples of this process is in the 're-discovery' of child sexual abuse as a significant social problem. What many social workers have found is that by choosing to work in this area, or even by being open to talk to their clients about these issues, they have felt, at one remove, the pressures that the survivors of the abuse have experienced – and, as with their clients they have also felt the considerable need for emotional support.

Practice Focus 5.1

A social worker who had just listened to a young adult's first disclosure of child sexual abuse returned to the office and the team room pale, shaking and extremely upset, unable to comprehend the reason for this state of emotion. She understood that, for other social workers who might have been abused as children such disclosures had the potential to be distressing – but where were her feelings coming from?

'I don't understand; I haven't been abused; why do I feel so bad?'

No matter how limited the similarity in experience between worker and client, the social worker in Practice Focus 5.1 was acutely aware of the emotional needs of her client and, by being open to her pain and her emotion, experienced that piece of work as enormously stressful.

As well as finding our clients' pain and emotion demanding, it is not surprising that such pain and emotion will sometimes find an echo in ourselves. Because social work deals with families, their relationships and their problems, it is perhaps inevitable that some cases will have a resonance for social workers of experiences in their own life. This resonance can become an extreme pressure, not least because there is sometimes a presumption that, by working with those cases, we can prove our ability to be detached from our own personal issues – and thereby prove our professional capability.

Practice Focus 5.2

A recently qualified social worker was trying to explain why his last placement had been so difficult:
  'It was my last placement before qualifying, it was very important to me that it went well. The placement that had been planned fell through at the last minute. There was a real shortage of alternatives and I felt forced to accept another placement in an area that I knew would be painful for me. Sure enough, all the old memories, all the old issues from my childhood came flooding back – I really struggled.'

Resistance and intractability

It is not uncommon, of course, for clients to show resistance to the intervention of the social worker, although this will tend to vary according to client group. Child protection is one field of social work in which the level of resistance can be very high, especially on the part of alleged perpetrators. This can have the effect of putting the locus of control outside the immediate sway of the practitioner.

  Resistance can manifest itself in a variety of ways. For example, service users who are suffering from stress may, and frequently do, display behaviours that can, in themselves, prove to be very demanding and a significant source of pressure for social work staff. As Morrison (1990) puts it: 'We work with some of the most damaged people in our society, whose suspicion, resentfulness, anger or despair is often vented on us as we try to help them' (p. 259).

For some social work clients, their periods of stress do not result in an end to their problems, and they may be caught in a cycle of stress that can lead them into more extreme forms of behaviour and thus to make more potentially stressful demands on the practitioners who are working with them. When these issues remain unresolved, behaviour that is even more stressful to the social worker can result.

In our study of three local authorities, 22 per cent of field social workers indicated that: 'the unchangeability of clients' problems by means within your power' caused them 'considerable' or 'extreme' stress. This and similar feelings of 'professional impotence' were associated with heightened levels of anxiety and depression in our sample. In a similar way, Fineman's (1985) study identified a particular type of client who was seen as being remarkably resistant to change: 'There were certain types of client who acted as a focus for the social worker's feelings of helplessness or failure – the "intractables". These were people for whom nothing seemed to work or could be done. They could depress a social worker who already felt trapped by the desire to "keep trying"' (p. 71). Here we have a 'Myth of Sisyphus' situation in which success seems highly unlikely but where, as a result of a court order for example, we are obliged to maintain our efforts against all the odds. This can be very disconcerting and can so easily lead to feelings of hopelessness and futility. Trying to do our best by our clients then becomes a very onerous task.

The breadth of the task

A further fundamental premise that needs to be taken into account is that the scope of the tasks and duties social workers undertake is extremely wide, as is the nature of social work as an occupational category. As the Barclay Committee (1982) pointed out:

Social work is a relatively young profession. It has grown rapidly as the flow of legislation has greatly increased the range and complexity of its work . . . Large departments have grown up in which social workers find it difficult to come to terms with the complex pressures which surround them (p. vii).

In effect, this means that social work practitioners potentially have to respond to a very diverse series of demands that they frequently have little power in shaping. This was reflected in Jones *et al.*'s (1991) study in which it was found that the fact of: 'Having a wide variety of tasks makes my job difficult' constituted a considerable demand for some workers. Even more interestingly perhaps, this stressor had a high positive correlation with reported levels of anxiety ($p < 0.001$).

Violence and aggression

No discussion about the potentially stressful nature of the social work task would be complete without reference to the effects of actual or threatened violence. During the 1980s three social workers in the UK were actually killed whilst undertaking their duties, and numerous more were subjected to severe assaults of various kinds that had physical, psychological and emotional consequences for the staff concerned. To some degree, this violence could be seen to reflect the stress to which the clients concerned are subject. This violence should also not be viewed purely on a personal or individual level. Violence needs to be seen as related to the structure of society in terms of wider social issues such as class exploitation and alienation, male power and dominance and racial oppression, points we shall touch on in Chapter 6.

In particular, it is important to remember that, in the main, it is women practitioners who deliver the social work service to the client – even though, interestingly, recent research has hinted that male staff may be more vulnerable to physical assault than their women colleagues (though, in our study, female social workers reported the threat of violence as an even greater source of pressure than did male staff). Having said this, we should also remember that, at the point of assault, the reasons underlying the act of violence may make little difference to how the practitioner experiences the assault. What is certain, though, is that, be it actual or threatened, verbal or physical, violence is likely to be acutely stressful for those who encounter it.

Practice Focus 5.3 (*Source*: Scott and Stradling, 1992)

Maureen was a field social worker who had recently been assaulted whilst visiting a couple who misused drugs. A neurological examination of Maureen revealed that the use of her right arm and leg was impeded in that she had lost the sensation of pressure in both, though she could move them voluntarily. The neurologist was unsure how quickly, if at all, the damage would be repaired. Maureen was prescribed daily physiotherapy, and had to wear a support collar for the damaged neck. In addition part of her head continued to feel numb. Maureen was referred to the counsellor four weeks after the assault. She had constant flashbacks to the day of the assault. She was reliving the whole scene as if it were conducted in slow motion, starting with the baby's blank gaze, the sight of Matt sprawled out on the settee, and Jane picking up the hairbrush and advancing towards her.

Not only does Maureen relive the scene of stress as though it were a slow-motion nightmare, but she finds her physical debility a constant reminder of the intrusion that she suffered, which causes her stress many weeks after the event.

Fineman (1985) remarks: 'Threat from clients could be directly physical in nature, as well as psychological. Not often were the social workers intimidated in this way, but when they were the experience was usually a memorable one' (p. 68).

Fineman's study actually took place between 1980 and 1982, but more recent empirical studies have suggested that violence as a stressor has become even more important to the majority of staff. For example, Gibson *et al.* (1989) discovered that almost 70 per cent of their sample were affected by the political violence in Ireland ('the troubles'). Similarly, within our own study, a sample drawn from three different British Social Services Departments reported that dealing with 'physically violent clients' and 'verbally abusive clients' came first and second, respectively, in terms of potential stress, from a series of 29 different social work tasks, with the former causing 'considerable' or 'extreme' stress to 50 per cent, and the latter to 46 per cent of workers. Also interesting was the fact that 'worry about physical attack' came only eleventh in the same series (although even this was considered a 'considerable' or 'extreme' stressor by 23 per cent). This could be seen to suggest that, whilst an actual assault is seen as a significant stressor, worry about the possibility of assault receives a far lower priority.

In Webb's (1989) research into stress in residential social work, 69 per cent of the sample reported physical violence as a stressor and the majority (70 per cent) of all the individual specific incidents that were reported involved physical violence. Jones *et al.* (1991) also found that the actuality of violent clients is far more stressful than the overall threat of violence. This study found a far higher occurrence of violence or threats of violence than did the earlier Fineman study: 'Threats of violence were a common experience – 56% of workers had experienced an "upsetting threat of violence" in the last two years. 38% had been threatened on two or more occasions' (p. 452).

This study also found that the higher the number of times a worker had experienced upsetting threats of violence, the higher the likelihood would be of that worker perceiving the threat of assault as a significant stressor. This would appear to contradict the common assumption that working in an area of high violence is likely to give some degree of immunity from the stress of such incidents. On the contrary, it would seem, exposure to threats of violence diminishes our ability to ignore the problem. The Hertfordshire study found that their 'high stress' group of staff were more likely than the 'low stress' group to have suffered actual assault or upsetting threats within the last two years. This leads us to speculate whether being under stress can actually make us more likely to be exposed to threats or actual violence.

The seeming differences between the Fineman study and the later empirical studies could suggest that either violence is becoming more common in social work, or it is increasingly being recognised as a problem. Whichever is correct, the stress factor remains high.

Practice Focus 5.4

A social worker on the way to a training course on violence to staff had to pass through the reception area of a Social Services office. The way was blocked by a young aggressive male, who asked "are you a social worker?" A reply in the affirmative was met by a punch in the face from the man, who then walked out of the office. The worker continued on to the training course in a state of confusion and was heard to ask the trainer whether this encounter had been 'set up' as a practical part of the course!

Quite simply this client had decided to vent his violence on a social worker. In the absence of one that he knew, any would do. The client's anger and assault left the worker in a state of upset and confusion – what had he done to deserve the assault? What was behind it? What could he have done to stop it? The worker's original, illogical hypothesis that the violence had been 'set up' as an experiential element within the course was perhaps a way of dealing with this confusion.

In recent years there has been an increased level of awareness of the potential for violence in social work and social care. However, we should not allow this to mislead us into thinking that there is a greater sensitivity to the impact of violence upon the workers concerned. The point is powerfully made by Hopkins (1987a): 'There is little reference in the current "violence training" to the impact of threatening behaviour. It focuses on the management of violence. The fact that another human being may hate you so much that they want to kill you, is something that you are expected to accept and to live with' (p. 14). It is clear, therefore, that our understanding of threats and violence as a stressor leaves a great deal of progress yet to be made.

Care or control?

It is a classic dilemma of social work that staff are frequently faced with contradictory requests, both to care for, and to control, their clients, to empower them and sometimes to behave in a way that could be seen as repressive or controlling. Although social work is recognised as one of the 'caring professions', it would be naive not to acknowledge that there is also a significant element of social control as, for example, in juvenile justice or child protection work. This can place social workers in a very difficult position, operating at the point of conflict between the needs of the individual client and the wider social concerns – they are, as Clarke (1988, p. 63) puts it, 'caught in the middle'.

Practice Focus 5.5

Frances was a social worker in a specialist juvenile justice team. She had worked with Laura, an adolescent girl in care, for about a year on issues of petty offending. As their relationship strengthened, Laura began to tell Frances about the severe abuse and exploitation that she had suffered in her family of origin. At the same time as this, Laura's offences of theft (from shops) and violence (towards other adolescents) became more serious.

The pressure from the juvenile justice system, and from her own system, to control this young person was very strong – even though this would mean her moving 'up the tariff' of possible court disposals. On the other hand, Frances's own training and influence from her colleagues who specialised in child protection led her to feel that, at this stage, Laura needed to feel cared for, rather than controlled.

Frances felt pulled in two opposite directions, with each 'camp' very critical of the other. Frances already felt very stressed by the task that had been given to her, but felt even more pressurised by the impossibility of resolving the two conflicting expectations of task outcome.

In a similar vein, Preston-Shoot and Braye (1991) include the following conflict in their list of stress factors in social work which need to be addressed: 'The themes of partnership, consumer choice, empowerment, knowledge-led and needs-led assessments, as cornerstones of service delivery, conflict with themes of social control, economy, resource-led services, agency policy, and defensiveness' (pp. 17–18).

In residential social work the dual demands of care and control can be particularly stressful. 'Caring versus policing' was particularly significant for the residential sample in our own research. As McDerment (1988) points out, this stressor can become particularly apparent in the relationship between the establishment and the community in which it is based: 'The immediate neighbourhood can also put pressure on staff and thus create stress. Pressure to contain people who wander or abscond, or who give rise to anxiety through unacceptable social behaviour or appearance, can have a most negative effect on staff morale and client welfare' (p. 62).

In the child protection field, a particularly thorny paradox is the duty to protect children from parental abuse at the same time as behaving in a non-intrusive way towards those very same parents. This is acknowledged by Philip Noyes in his discussion of child protection inquiry reports:

Double standards operate in the field of child protection. Many of the inquiries note the difficulties in, and complexities of, social work tasks. The final submission to the Cleveland inquiry of the Social Services Department pointed out 'the Social Services, of course, always have a thankless task. If they are overcautious and take children away from their families they are pilloried for doing so. If they do not take the child away from the family and something terrible happens to the child, then likewise they are pilloried' (DOH, 1991a, p. 4).

This is a clear illustration of the 'no-win' situation for social workers caught on the horns of the care versus control dilemma. And, of course, because of the very nature of the social work enterprise, it is a dilemma which will remain with us in one shape or another.

The work environment

The work environment can be divided into two distinct components. The first of these, the office or work-base environment, was mentioned in Chapters 1 and 3, and will feature again in Chapter 6. It is an aspect that is amenable to change and is within the purview of management. The second, relatively under-researched, aspect of the work environment for social workers relates to the localities they so frequently visit, the communities in which they operate. Due to the poverty and powerlessness of so many of the families and individuals who become service users, the environments in which they live are often bleak, depressing, lacking in amenities and possibly violent.

Practice Focus 5.6

Sandra had a child care caseload and worked within a very poor estate in a town in the north of England. Besides the general atmosphere of the estate, Sandra found that she was doing most of her work on what was probably the most deprived road and adjoining cul-de-sac on the estate. It seemed that she knew every family in this small area. She could not remain unnoticed on any of her visits, and enjoyed a particularly poor relationship with the family who lived in the corner house. She began to find the whole environment very threatening. She dreaded having to make visits to the area and found herself frequently making excuses not to go.

There are, of course, strong and clear links between poverty, deprivation and social work. Being exposed to poverty is, of course, far less stressful than the situation of those who live in poverty. However, the frustration of knowing that poverty lies at the heart of so many of the problems social workers are trying to resolve, is a constant source of pressure, especially when staff realise how relatively powerless they are to tackle such structural or politically-based problems. Indeed, 'the knowledge that more resources would largely remedy a client's problems' was a source of 'considerable' or 'extreme' stress to 39 per cent of our sample.

Unsocial hours

A stressor that is particularly relevant to residential social workers is that of being obliged to work irregular, unsocial hours in order to provide 24 hour cover for their clients. This particular stressor is powerful in its own right but can, unfortunately, also be very effective in cutting down the practitioners' access to support from home. In our study, demands on home and social life, the difficulty of dividing home and work time and the lack of emotional support at home were particularly important for residential social work staff. Webb (1989) in his study of residential workers raised similar concerns: 'Almost 50% of questionnaires returned made mention of pressure being generated through home and work conflict. This was reportedly as a result of the unsocial hours required or feelings of being "trapped" in work when family or friends were in the pub' (p. 10).

Although fieldworkers do not face the same pressures of shiftwork rotas, the necessity of doing evening, or even weekend, work is very much a reality for the majority of social workers. Only 13 per cent of our sample of field social workers saw 'out of office hours visits' as causing them no stress. And, of course, such unsocial hours are usually worked in addition to normal office hours, with many staff not finding the time to reclaim the 'time off in lieu' to which they are entitled. For all categories of staff, working unsocial hours cuts down opportunities to relax, to socialise, to plan ahead or maintain regular social activities. In short, unsocial hours are not only a stressor in their own right but they also act as a barrier to relaxation and other forms of fending off stress.

Conclusion

What this chapter has shown is that there are many aspects of social work that make it an intrinsically pressurised job. However, this is not to say that it is intrinsically a stressful job. For, as we have noted, stress is a person's response to an inappropriate level of pressure. In terms of preventing or minimising social work stress, this gives us two avenues forward to explore – first, in relation to what is an appropriate level of pressure and, second, in relation to our response to that pressure.

Appropriate levels of pressure

An appropriate level of pressure is one that is within the capabilities of our coping methods – it is a level we are able to manage without losing control or without experiencing undue tension. In terms of dealing with stress, this means that we should take whatever steps are possible to ensure that we are not exposed to excessive levels of pressure. This entails looking at ways in which the stress factors outlined above can be reduced and guarded against, bearing in mind that it is highly unlikely that they will be removed or eliminated altogether.

Such ways would include:

- keeping uncertainty to a minimum, for example, by careful planning and appropriate use of information resources
- minimising the risk of aggression and violence through developing our interpersonal skills and so on
- avoiding getting stuck in the care versus control dilemma by, for example, being clear about our mandate to safeguard children in child protection cases (Dale *et al.*, 1986)

These, and other measures like them, are by no means foolproof. For example, no amount of interpersonal skill will prevent violence in some situations. However, measures such as these do help to cut down the level of risk and therefore the level of pressure. Time spent analysing one's own work situation and strategies for reducing pressure (and/or enhancing coping skills, increasing levels of support and so on) will be time well spent.

Response

As we have seen, stress is not simply an 'objective' matter but also has a significant subjective dimension. How we perceive our pressures, how we respond to them, will play a major part in determining whether or not pressure spills over into stress, whether the level of pressure outstrips our coping resources. How we respond will depend on a number of elements, including the following major components:

- expectations
- confidence/self-esteem
- support

It is worth spending some time considering each of these in turn. Our expectations are of central importance in so far as they dictate, to a large extent, how we will judge success or failure. That is, we may be setting ourselves up to fail by having unreasonably high expectations of what can be achieved. It may therefore be necessary to lower our sights and expect to achieve less in those areas outlined in this chapter. For example, if we try too hard to take away the uncertainty and unpredictability of social work, not only are we ultimately doomed to failure but also, we may be missing out on:

- developing the coping skills necessary for dealing with uncertainty (for example, flexibility)
- experiencing some degree of unpredictability as positive (that is, exciting and challenging)

Our expectations will influence the attitude we adopt to our pressures and so unrealistic expectations can stand in the way of adopting a positive and constructive attitude. That is, inappropriate expectations will prevent us from reframing the situation in a positive and manageable way.

Confidence and self-esteem can be seen to play a similar role. If we have little confidence in our ability to change what can be changed or accept what cannot, once again we are setting ourselves up to fail. Being able to distinguish between what is amenable to change and what must be accepted as inevitable depends, as we have seen, on having the wisdom to judge the extent to which our actions can have an impact. A lack of confidence will tend to bias our judgements in a negative direction, as we will tend to underestimate the degree of our power and influence.

The intrinsic stressors we have discussed in this chapter are amenable to some degree of change and influence but within certain limitations due to their very nature as, for example, with the tension between care and control. Thus, the task to be achieved for successful stress management is to establish a balance. On the one hand, we must not expect too much – as the inherent constraints will ultimately frustrate us – but, on the other, we must have faith in our ability to achieve some degree of change for, without this, we are undermining our own potential. As the Chinese proverb puts it, we may not be able to prevent the birds of sorrow from flying over us, but we can stop them making a nest in our hair.

This brings us to the third component, that of support. Maintaining the balance of avoiding the two extremes of idealistic expectations and a low level of confidence is a difficult task. It is one which benefits considerably from sharing the problem. It is very helpful, in dealing with matters such as these, to have the support of colleagues and line manager. These issues can legitimately feature on the agenda for team or staff meetings or for supervision sessions. But the question of support is more generally applicable to this area of stress management. Support is essential not only in terms of achieving this difficult balance but also with regard to coping with pressures in general, as was suggested in Chapter 2. The issue of support will be considered in more detail in Chapter 6 and so we will not discuss it further here.

It is no exaggeration to say that the area of 'intrinsic stressors' is a complex and intricate one, but we hope that the discussions here have helped to cast some light on the main issues. Also, of equal importance, we hope that the points raised will help to generate ideas about practical steps that can be taken to deal with the problems. We shall return to the issue of practical strategies in Chapter 7. First, however, we need to consider the extrinsic stressors in social work, that is, the ones that are not an inherent part of the social work task. This, then, is the subject matter of Chapter 6.

6

The Organisational Context

Pottage and Evans (1992) argue that: 'A shift from the traditional view of stress as a personal problem located in individuals, towards seeing it as an indicator of the ineffectiveness of work environments, systems and practices is necessary' (pp. 12–13). This is very much in line with the perspective we have adopted here, based on the view that stress is both an individual problem and an organisational one. Indeed, as our discussions in Chapter 4 suggested, we would even go so far as to say that it is a social and political matter. This chapter therefore examines those aspects of stress which are related to the organisations in which social work staff work. In particular, the focus is on those factors within the organisational context which, depending on how they are handled, can either assist staff in dealing with their pressures, or actually contribute to making those pressures overspill into stress. As McDerment (1988) points out: 'Organizational contributors to individual suffering cannot be emphasised enough' (p. 44).

The issues we are concerned with are those of workload, supervision, training, organisational culture and so on. These are the extrinsic aspects of social work. Unlike the intrinsic factors discussed in Chapter 5, these are the problems of social work which can be resolved, a point supported by the research of Jones *et al.* (1991): 'the items which correlated with psychological strain were not necessarily inherent features of the job related to dealing with clients, but were frequently peripheral features which could be remedied' (p. 465).

It is not a matter of minimising the effects of these factors or learning to adjust to them, although these tactics may be necessary in the short term. It is, rather, a matter of seeking to resolve or eliminate these problems by helping to create a supportive and constructive work environment. This is, in effect, the crux of human resource management – developing management structures, values and practices that enable staff to obtain maximum job satisfaction at minimum personal cost. This approach recognises that it is in the interests of organisations and their managers to safeguard the well-being of their staff. Where organisations fail in this respect, it is both the individuals and the organisations themselves that will suffer.

This chapter therefore seeks to address the question of how successful social work organisations are in promoting a positive work context for their staff and what improvements need to be instituted. It explores the organisational context or work system and the ways in which it supports or undermines the efforts and endeavours of staff.

There are two distinct but interwoven elements within this work system:

1. How does the system organise tasks, prioritise them and allocate them to individual workers and their teams? That is, how are work pressures organised, distributed and managed?
2. What staff support systems exist? How appropriate and effective are they? What gaps or inadequacies are there?

Both of these elements will be relevant to our discussions in the remainder of this chapter. We shall begin with a topic which has a very close and significant relationship with stress, that of workload.

Workload

In Jones *et al.*'s (1991) study, the issue of workload was of crucial importance:

The highest perceived demands were to do with having too much work. In response to the statement 'I have more work than I have time to do', 74% either agreed or strongly agreed. A similar number (73%) either agreed or strongly agreed to the statement 'I often have to work extra hours to get my work done'. . . Half the sample (50%) felt under constant pressure to take on more work (p. 453).

In a similar vein, Fineman (1985) recalls some of the comments that his sample made concerning workload: 'The sheer quantity, and sometimes quality, of the perceived workload was of particular significance: "My main stresses came with too much work – can't look at it all, allocate it all – it starts building up." were the comments of one of the managers in the group' (p. 46). In our study, 'time pressure' was a significant source of stress to social work staff, with 39 per cent reporting that it caused them 'considerable' or 'extreme' stress. In addition, in McDerment's (1988) study of residential and day care staff in the south of England, workload also figured as a significant stressor. Participants specified long hours, being alone on duty, and lack of time to do the work according to their own standards as being particularly distressing. There is therefore no shortage of research evidence to link issues of workload with pressure and stress.

Of course, it is not simply a matter of the amount of work. The nature of the workload a practitioner carries can also be a major factor in increasing or reducing pressure. This could mean that a particular client group or specialist field may generate higher levels of pressure than others. On the one hand, Fineman (1985) claims that a child protection caseload, mentioned by almost all in his study, had the potential to be particularly stressful. On the other hand, however, other studies have failed to identify significant differences based on type of caseload.

A further issue that could be especially significant is the potential difference between a specialist and a generic caseload. On the face of it, the specialist caseload would seem to have several advantages over the generic one. These would include:

- specialisation could bring greater expertise and confidence in a given field, a factor which could significantly increase coping abilities
- the sheer variety of work within a generic caseload might, in itself, be seen as a source of pressure; as we saw in Chapter 5, 'having a wide variety of tasks makes my job difficult' was ranked as the nineteenth most stressful job demand in the Jones *et al.* (1991) study

However, before becoming convinced of the efficacy of the specialist caseload as a means of dealing with stress, it would be wise to remember that, paradoxically, the variety of tasks and situations that a generic caseload involves could actually bring relief from stress for many workers. For example, in our study, 'amount of variety in your job' was rated as a source of job satisfaction by 75 per cent of our sample. What suits one group of workers does not automatically suit others. For example, in one survey, Murphy (1991) reported an extremely high degree of stress in a small, highly specialised, experienced team in north-west England – in spite of all the advantages of specialisation and experience that the team seemed to enjoy.

Even within a specialism, staff can be further channelled into a much more narrowly defined specialist area, with little chance of working outside that limited sphere. For example, child protection duties have frequently 'squeezed out' other types of work with children and families – this is what Stevenson (1991) has called the 'cuckoo' effect of child protection work. In one of the local authorities studied as part of our research, many staff commented that fieldwork services for children and families had almost completely been taken over by child protection work, as the following comment from a social work manager illustrates: 'What you have to realise is that, in this area, if you haven't abused your child you don't get a service.'

This reflects a general feeling in many quarters of social work that the tasks are getting increasingly harder, the expectations increasingly higher. This is partly recognised in the following comment from Pottage and Evans (1992): 'The outcome of the current service culture is an over ambitious expectation and demand on human resources, which infects all working, training and development systems. There is a marked discrepancy between expectation and actual capacity: a classic feature of stress' (p. 13).

In residential social work, these themes have been outlined in the Department of Health Guidance on the Children Act 1989 (Volume 4):

The way in which children's homes are used in the care of children has changed greatly in recent years. Whilst residential solutions are used less frequently overall, the young people in the homes are older than before and are older than other young people in care. Placements are frequently of short duration and some are made at critical times when other arrangements are changing or have broken down (DOH, 1991b, p. 1).

The message is clear – the reduction in numbers of children and young people in residential care has been more than matched by an increase in the difficulty of client and client behaviour. The guidance then goes on to attempt to establish a whole new set of standards for residential care. Not only is difficulty increased, but also the expectations of work to be done and outcomes to be achieved are considerably raised: 'The Act and Regulations, as well as the guidance, make significant demands on those responsible for children's homes, and it is hoped that new legislative provisions will help bring about important improvements in the level of service provided in homes' (DOH, 1991b, p. 1).

In field social work, the most apparent example of increased difficulty and increased expectation is in the field of child protection work. Although the current phase of child protection social work began relatively recently, the difficulty of the typical child protection case has increased considerably, and expectations in terms of the protection of child, agency and parents have also grown significantly. This raises the issue of resources, a significant dimension of workload and its pressures. One of the intrinsic stressors of social work additional to those covered in Chapter 5 is the conflict of potentially infinite demand for services matched against finite resources. This has produced, in recent years, a strong emphasis on efficiency, attempting to maximise the results obtained from available human and material resources. Whilst few would doubt the wisdom of cutting out waste and encouraging resourcefulness, there is, none the less, a strong feeling amongst many social work staff that expectations of what can be done on a limited budget have become increasingly unrealistic. This feeling is very neatly captured by the parable of the peasant's donkey:

The Peasant's Donkey

The peasant owned a hard-working donkey. Unfortunately, it was proving too expensive to keep. One day the peasant decided to economise by reducing the donkey's feed. All went well. After two months the donkey was down to half of what it usually ate; after three months, to one quarter, but just when the donkey seemed to have got the hang of it, and had become accustomed, by the fourth month, to eating nothing at all, it died.

Some agencies have attempted to make this message clear to the political hierarchy whilst at the same time reluctantly agreeing to resource reductions: 'The stress levels associated with budgetary reductions are considerable. This is particularly so when there are substantial other changes forthcoming, as in new legislation. The negative consequences of this in terms of staff absence through sickness and loss of personal effectiveness are well known' (extract from a 'Policy Options 1992/1993' document from an English Local Authority Social Services Department).

The 'Pindown Experience' (Levy and Kahan, 1991) in which residential care staff were heavily criticised for using control methods which involved depriving children of rights and basic liberties has clearly shown that what happened was not the result of a group of sadistic or abusive workers coming together to harm children, but the result of a grossly under-resourced staff group, subjected to the strains of a great deal of reorganisation, having to cope with an increasingly demanding group of clients. As the report puts it: 'Providing a quality service requires an understanding of the children's needs . . . and the kinds of resources and supports which are essential to meet them' (p. 161). The report goes on to criticise the welcoming and acceptance of 'cheap remedies' to social work problems. It therefore serves to highlight how an under-resourced service can produce disastrous results.

In field social work this lack of resources to do an increasingly difficult job was clearly demonstrated by the Gibson *et al.* (1989) study where 'experiencing too little time to perform duties to your satisfaction' and 'rationing of scarce services or resources' were the two most frequently mentioned sources of stress. Although the process of setting priorities is, at one level, an effective strategy for managing workload and its attendant pressures, where demand for services far outstrips supply, 'prioritisation' can seem an inadequate short-term remedy which is only storing up problems for the future. Richards *et al.* (1990) make a similar point when they argue that:

Where bombardment is heavy and resources clearly inadequate, even the most "effective" workload management may be ineffective. The rationing of cases and of time can be justified at an intellectual level; but they may fail to resolve the moral dilemmas which are produced, or to raise morale or address how people really feel about their work (p. 20).

Also worth mentioning under the heading of workload and resources is the issue of staff shortages. Although there is still some inevitable degree of movement of staff within social work, added to a constant flow of people moving into (and frequently out of) the field, this only accounts for one part of the staff shortage situation. Where agencies use the not uncommon expedient of reducing costs by leaving posts unfilled, this may be effective in financial terms, but is potentially disastrous in terms of work pressures and staff morale.

There are many other aspects of workload which could usefully bear further analysis but space does not permit extending our discussions further. What has, we hope, been established is that workload is a very significant issue in relation to pressure and stress. Attempts to achieve effective stress management therefore need to have workload high on their agenda.

Bureaucracy versus professionalism

Modern management theory is geared towards moving beyond traditional bureaucracy to a more flexible and responsive approach as is shown by the following passage from Storey (1992), where he comments on the Audit Commission's insistence that:

> bureaucracy is no longer an appropriate organisational mode for today's environment. What is currently required, it suggests, is flexibility and responsiveness. An example of its thinking is its publication Good Management in Local Government (Audit Commission, 1985). The emphasis is on the management of change 'rather than administering standstill or growth'. It talks of developing a 'vision' and deriving from this strategies, plans and budgets. These are to be followed up with systems for performance review (p. 52).

If this is to be believed, we are moving towards an era of 'post-bureaucracy' in which the devolution of responsibility will produce a greater emphasis on professional judgement and less on hierarchical control. In terms of stress, this is a very significant departure as it raises the significance of issues of professionalism and control.

Control, or lack of control, on the part of the worker over the work process, is a significant potential stressor. In simple terms, the more control the worker is allowed over the process, the less stressed he or she is likely to feel by that very process. In our study, 'freedom to choose your own method of working' was the second highest source of job satisfaction (just behind 'fellow workers'), with 79 per cent satisfied with 'the amount of responsibility given' in their job. Unfortunately, some research has suggested that little control or professional discretion is left to the basic grade worker. Howe (1986a) claims that true control is now vested in the distant welfare manager: 'The effect of management-based techniques gaining control is not just that control by social workers is reduced but that the content of the work is prescribed both explicitly (through authority-based directives) and implicitly (by managerial design and structure)' (p. 126).

Similarly, Gibson *et al.* (1989) found that: 'Over ninety per cent of respondents said they felt unable to influence decisions at least sometimes and almost one third said this was the case often or always. Eighty seven per cent said they felt powerless to change unsatisfactory situations' (p. 8). One possible explanation for this result was that the sample was relatively young and inexperienced – perhaps more experience would lead to greater control. Unfortunately, however, Murphy (1991) suggests that, in some areas of work, even very experienced staff are denied this control:

The most commonly identified and strongest stressor was work process or, more accurately, the lack of control over that work process . . . [A]lthough the team was brought into the investigation because of its professional knowledge and skill, once the task had begun this was nullified by the strict hierarchical control over the process which seemed to cut them off from their professional skill base (p. 13).

Within this area of control, it is clear that there are a number of levels that can actively remove the control over the work process from the basic grade worker – the governmental or legislative level that shapes expectations of service and overall allocation of resources; the agency level (for example, senior managers and elected members) where policies are determined; and the line management hierarchy where the direction and focus of practice are supervised.

There is an argument that these layers of control should be a comfort and a help to social workers: 'At the same time this very lack of autonomy offers a degree of protection – or should do' (Stone, 1990, p. 46). However, Pottage and Evans (1992) offer a different perspective:

> Our analysis illustrates the problems of over-reliance on prescription and hierarchical relationships, so that organisations are unable to learn from their own experience. In so doing they diminish the significance of individual workers and the issues they face, and as an outcome fail to maximise the talent at their disposal (p. 31).

Similarly, Hackman and Oldham (1980) argue that many workers have a 'development orientation' and look for challenge, growth and responsibility in their work. Where such workers are afforded sufficient responsibility and autonomy, their responses can be seen to be much more positive and thus of more value to the organisation. The parallels with social work should be fairly easy to draw.

Although few social workers might want to claim full 'professional' autonomy, many would want to enjoy a greater amount of appropriate discretion over the task. It would seem that a department or a team that attempted to give back some level of control over the task to the worker, would affect considerably the perceived levels of pressure within the agency.

The administrative tasks and procedural controls that the organisation uses to process the workload can in themselves constitute a considerable source of pressure for those who have to comply with them. Even though those same organisational processes are intended at one level to make the task more manageable, in practice they are usually seen as an extra job demand or stressor. In a similar way, the procedural systems designed to process work in an efficient way can be perceived as being oppressive and stressful. Corby (1989) has pointed out that: 'Social workers' perceptions of the child abuse system vary, but many are suspicious of the way in which it operates. The system is clearly seen by some to be oppressive' (p. 59). In Gibson *et al.*'s (1989) study in the north of Ireland, 46 per cent of staff found that 'administrative responsibilities' were a source of moderate or high levels of stress.

In Hertfordshire 'I have to devote too much of my time to paperwork and administration' was one of the highest demands that staff reported: 'The amount of paper wᴏᵣk would seem to be an important component of work overload, 76 per cent of respondents agreeing that they had to devote too much time to paperwork and administration' (Jones *et al.*, 1991, p. 453).

It is clear that, at one level, practitioners may resent the actual work entailed in administrative processes and procedural systems but, of equal importance, these elements may be seen as another method of hierarchical control which becomes stressful by removing the locus of control over work from the practitioner.

The physical environment

Although it is difficult to control the environment in clients' homes and communities (as was discussed in Chapter 5), it should be possible for the organisation to have control over the physical standards that exist in work bases. In our study, 60 per cent of field social workers from the three authorities were dissatisfied with their working conditions. It is clear, though, that there can be considerable variation in physical environment even within agencies. Whereas good physical amenities could be seen as a form of staff support, poor environment (usually evidenced by the lack of space, light, heat and so on) acts as an extra stressor or job demand.

Practice Focus 6.1

In a small-scale study of stress in an experienced team, the group found that, despite coping with a highly pressurised work task and having considerable experience of potentially stressful situations, the poor work environment (and in particular the lack of work space) proved to be a considerable source of pressure.

This could mean that, where a team or individual is already under a great deal of pressure, the physical

> environment can serve to exacerbate that stress. It is also important to consider that a poor working environment can be a considerable stressor in its own right.

A poor working environment gives a strong impression that staff are not valued and are not worthy of even a limited investment in creating a helpful and pleasant atmosphere in which to undertake their difficult tasks. The net result can be a demoralised group of staff whose effectiveness can be blunted by the sense of adversity and demotivation a poor working environment can so easily generate.

Practice Focus 6.2

The area office housed several fieldwork teams. The general level of environment and amenities in the office was poor, but more worryingly, because of the frequency with which windows were broken, and the poor repair service, the teams on the ground floor had reduced access, or occasionally no access at all, to natural light. Not surprisingly, the atmosphere in those particular team rooms was even more pressured than in the rest of the building; arguments were more frequent and 'fun' very difficult to discover

---

Support systems

We also need to consider those elements of the organisational system that specifically seek to help the staff involved in service delivery. These are the work elements which can immediately affect the worker's subjective negative response to a given work demand. These are the elements that McDerment (1988) has labelled 'organisational resources':

Organisational resources are support from a supervisor and colleagues and strong team work. Good teamwork for residential social workers develops from effective meetings in which work problems are clarified and experience and knowledge are shared. This promotes participation in a caring, sharing organisation (McDerment, 1988, p. 148).

However, what McDerment failed to deal with in this section was the fact that the 'caring, sharing' elements in the social work organisation are in constant conflict with the macho, task-orientated culture that urges workers to 'be tough' and ignore issues of stress. As Morrison (1990) puts it: 'Unfortunately when it comes to myths and beliefs around the management of stress, many of the most fundamental survival messages have been along the lines of "don't feel, be strong, don't admit mistakes and coping is professional"' (p. 255).

Appraisal and supervision

As with all the subject areas within this section, appraisal and supervision would naturally seem to form a crucial part of a staff support system. However, the message throughout this section will be that if well performed, all parts of the staff care dimension could be vital ingredients of a supportive work context, but if lacking or poorly performed, then each part can add to perceived stress.

The three essential ingredients of supervision (whether undertaken singly or in groups) are:

- *Standard setting.* Where amount, standard and type of the practitioner's work are reviewed, to see if they meet desired criteria and required levels of performance.
- *Staff development.* This is the part of the process that is largely educational. It enquires what knowledge, skills and values the member of staff may need in order to maintain and improve standards. The process of supervision is helpful in this respect, both directly (by providing learning opportunities) and indirectly (by identifying training needs).
- *Staff care.* This is the element of the process where the supervisor enquires – What professional/personal issues are

preventing you from achieving your optimal level of performance? Can I or the organisation help with these?

As long as these three elements are kept in proportion then the process of supervision will be an effective means of staff support. However, when the standard-setting ingredient begins to displace the other two (as it has a tendency to do) then the affected staff could experience the whole process as an additional pressure (see Morrison, 1993, for a fuller discussion of these issues).

Practice Focus 6.3

John had been a member of the team for three years, and was going through a particularly difficult period. The new team leader was quite worried about the standard of work that John was producing, and spent much time in supervision checking and questioning the detail of John's work and case recording. John became increasingly alienated from the process and seemed to spend most of his time avoiding supervision. The quality of John's work decreased; he became increasingly exhausted and cynical, and began to find the simplest of decisions difficult to make. After a particularly difficult interview with a verbally aggressive client, John went on long-term sick leave and did not return to social work.

Where the crucial elements of staff support, such as supervision, are turned completely towards the interests of the organisation, rather than the interests of the individual worker, the strain can become severe.

Appraisal, if used appropriately, plays a similar role to that of supervision. It contributes to maintaining or establishing high quality practice by providing constructive feedback – providing opportunities for overcoming weaknesses and building on strengths. In this way, it can be a significant source of support by offering scope for personal and professional development as well as a safety net to guard against bad practice. It therefore has the potential to make a key contribution to high morale and motivation. However, as with supervision, if it is used simply as a means of 'checking up' on the workforce, it can easily become an additional pressure – an organisational strength becomes a weakness and a further burden for staff to bear.

Team support

Fineman (1985) provides an example of one team leader who had succeeded in establishing a supportive team atmosphere: 'his integrative meetings with staff on professional matters . . . were probably critical ingredients in helping to set the supportive climate . . . they talked of a basically comfortable atmosphere in the team and a freedom to move in a number of different directions' (p. 106). But this ideal of a supportive team environment, although extremely effective in reducing pressures and promoting good practice, is not seen as typical by Fineman. He claims that the team meeting is a good barometer of the team's supportive climate: 'Any esprit de corps fast gave way to in-fighting, games and ploys, and the ritual of personal agendas would soon swamp the formal agenda. The tension in meetings was overwhelming for some in the present study – they would withdraw psychologically and seek excuses not to attend' (p. 160).

The team or staff group can be seen as an essential element in staff support. But, if the formal team fails to meet its members' needs, then a number of informal supportive groupings can emerge: 'These were highly valued informal pairings and sub-groups which cut across and sometimes supplanted the roles of formal supervision and team meetings' (Fineman, 1985, p. 161).

In residential social work this element of team support is, if anything, even more important than in fieldwork. In our own study 'conflict with colleagues' was a particularly significant stressor for the residential social work sample. McDerment (1988) states that, in the exploratory studies used in her text:

'lack of team work, expressed in staff conflict, inadequate peer support and an unsupportive atmosphere, emerged as the major stressors . . . In residential and day care, this desire for good teamwork and team support is paramount. The very nature of group care requires the development of a team' (p. 154). It is clear that, because of the particular nature of the residential social work task, the lack of team support would not only reduce the level of staff support but would constitute a major stressor for the staff concerned.

Training and development

One element frequently overlooked in an organisation's provision of staff care is the role of training and development. At its simplest, training is an essential staff support in so far as it seeks (along with supervision and appraisal) to enable staff to undertake and understand the social work task. The code of practice for staff care in the Health and Social Services (Centre for Occupational Studies, 1991) states that: 'The Training Department of an organisation is often addressing care needs of staff through training work, implicitly and without formal recognition of the fact. Such work should be made explicit and legitimised as an integral part of the total planned staff care provision.'

Training is geared towards helping staff carry out their duties and develop relevant skills for present or future demands. However, as far as future demands are concerned, many social work staff have no preparatory training prior to taking up post. Residential staff – most often women – are expected to be able to reproduce their 'natural' caring ability, very often without the benefit of an adequate induction period or pre-work training. This applies to staff working with children and young people, despite government guidelines: 'Education and training are not luxuries; it is essential that all members of staff working in child protection are properly trained for the jobs which they are expected to do' (DOH, 1991c, p. 54).

Of course, it may also be highly appropriate for training to take its staff care role even more seriously, for example, by including elements of self-care and stress management within training courses with all levels of staff.

Counselling

Counselling is the element of the organisational system that recognises that no matter how well organised there is always the risk that a proportion of staff in any department experience such extreme levels of stress that they would benefit from an input of an independent counsellor, experienced in staff care issues. This is the part of any staff support system that is reactive rather than proactive but, even though used after a practitioner has been badly effected by stress, it can still be seen as basically a positive provision that can help people manage their stress constructively and return to work in a positive frame of mind.

It is ironic that a service which relies so heavily on the efficacy of individual helping should be reluctant to use such a form of help to aid its own staff . Ready access to counselling services is still not the norm within social work. Some authors (Hemsley, 1986; Murphy, 1991) have commented on practitioners' seeming reluctance to avail themselves of counselling help. But, at the same time, that this reluctance reflects the 'be tough' culture of some teams and agencies (Wiener, 1989; Murphy, 1991).

The working party which produced the staff care code of practice for Health and Social Services staff referred to above suggested that counselling schemes are part of the reactive element of staff care which are activated when other proactive elements have failed to alleviate an individual's stress. However, Harper and Murphy (1993) suggest that this separation from the mainstream is instrumental in discouraging the use of such services. Furthermore, they argue that it is only when the culture of a team or staff group, reflected in the active encouragement of the manager, shows that it values individual counselling that such help will be appropriately used. It is only when counselling becomes accepted as an integral part of the way an organisation operates that this part of the staff care service will become acceptable to practitioners.

Organisational culture

In sociological terms, culture is defined as 'shared ways of seeing, thinking and doing'. This is broadly applicable to organisational culture, although there are two main 'camps' in terms of how the concept is used in practice. The first approach sees culture as a quality of the organisation – something an organisation 'has' – and which can be changed or opposed by management. The alternative view sees culture as what the organisation 'is' – the sum total of the values, beliefs and ideologies of the people who make up the organisation. As such, it cannot be changed by management edict but has to be 'crafted' (Mintzberg, 1988), carefully shaped and moulded through negotiation and skilled human resource management.

Culture sets up, through patterns of interaction between staff, a set of shared meanings and expectations, a common orientation towards the work task, the organisation and the wider work context. However, set against this, are a range of 'sub-cultures', patterns which differ from work group to work group (for example, between field and residential workers) or even between teams within the same building. Culture is therefore a complex and multifaceted entity and one to which social work staff, particularly managers, would do well to devote some of their attention.

An organisation's culture can be a supportive one which promotes good staff care or, sadly, it can be a negative and destructive influence which generates additional pressure where it should be generating support. This is particularly the case where a negative culture of helplessness develops:

> certain cultural orientations have an important psychological impact, producing a sense of futility and pessimism in people long before they enter the problem-solving arena. The culture induces a situation similar to Seligman's 'learned helplessness' (1975) – a psychological state which results when a person perceives that he can no longer control his own destiny. If this perception finds confirmation in experience – if one learns from trying that one is indeed helpless – 'this saps the motivation to initiate responses' (Seligman,

1975, p. 74). In other words one simply gives up trying; the energy and will to resolve problems and attain goals drains away. (Bate, 1992, pp. 228–9)

Where this point has been reached, stress can never be far away. The pressures of work are not counterbalanced by motivation and commitment. Consequently, workers find that their batteries are not being recharged – they are not being energised by their work and the environment in which it takes place. It is not surprising, therefore, that staff soon find themselves operating on reserve supplies of energy and thus prone to disillusion, exhaustion and stress. The relationship between organisational culture and stress is therefore an important one but, unfortunately, one to which we are unable to devote sufficient space to do it justice. Note, however, that our earlier discussions of gender and of the masculine 'be tough' attitude to pressure are also very relevant to this concept of organisational culture.

Structure and organisational change

In recent years the extent of major organisational change within social work agencies has been highly significant, and shows no sign of diminishing. Partly as a response to major legislative change and partly as a response to the enforced reduction in resources (as in the story of the Peasant's Donkey), major reorganisational change in both statutory and voluntary sectors has been very much in vogue. Fineman (1985) hinted that social work staff could try to develop an immunity to reorganisation and that this manifested itself in a 'cutting off' reaction: 'So many changes have been planned and nothing has happened. I just shut off – ignore it. I get on with my job' (p. 11).

However, there were many more staff who were unable to cope in this way:

Those who were unable to cope in this way were more specifically threatened by the change. They expressed fears about what lay ahead and the good things they might lose especially supportive colleagues and comfortable working relationships . . . Few social workers felt adequately consulted or involved in the process (p. 11).

In our study, staff in one agency which had reorganised twelve months previously reported that the majority of field and residential staff felt inadequately consulted and had suffered undue stress as a result of the reorganisation changes and the way they had been managed.

One clear consequence of major reorganisations is the removal, for basic grade and lower management staff, of control over their work. Consequently, lack of consultation becomes even more important, especially as reorganisations threaten to remove those elements of staff support that the worker has come to rely upon in dealing with stress (that is, work environment, team support, supervision and so on).

Most worrying of all perhaps, our own study found that, within the one agency that had undergone a major reorganisation, the staff were likely to be experiencing their work tasks or job demands as being far more stressful than their colleagues in other social work agencies within the sample. Also of concern was the fact that this group contained a significantly higher proportion of staff who were suffering from serious (health-affecting) anxiety.

Management theory places a great deal of faith in the power of restructuring organisations in order to improve their effectiveness (particularly their cost-effectiveness) but, regrettably, it would seem that the human costs of such reorganisations have been paid inadequate attention. Restructuring has been seen as a ready solution to a range of organisational problems without the full impact being given adequate consideration. Morrison *et al.* (1987) describe the problem in the following terms: 'There may be a shared or managerial fantasy that problems are always the result of organisational defects, and therefore that reorganisation is always the solution. Often this occurs when managers and teams do not listen to each other and solutions are invoked before the real problem is clarified' (p. 10).

It is to be hoped that the fashion for major reorganisational changes will have a limited lifespan as the costs of this drastic form of problem-solving become increasingly recognised. Alternatively, managers, it is hoped, will learn from their experience of reorganisations and will ensure that they are handled more sensitively and constructively in future.

Conclusion

When talking about the place of the organisation within social work stress, it is important to remember that, where not attempting to help with that stress, the organisation may be exacerbating it. Indeed, we could even go so far as to say that there is no neutral middle ground; an employing organisation's policies and practices will either help or hinder its workforce in carrying out their day to day duties. Where they help, this will be experienced as supportive. Where they hinder, this will be experienced not only as a lack of support, but also as a source of pressure in its own right. Failing to support staff is therefore a very costly proposition for social work organisations as it means that their most important resource – their staff – are being worn down rather than fired up.

The organisation has three main points of control over pressure and stress. These are:

1. The allocation of work.
2. Staff care policies (based in reality not rhetoric).
3. Its overall approach to its staff.

All three of these are important aspects of human resource management and, as Smith (1992) puts it: 'the evidence suggests that investment in human resources is one of the most effective investments that organisations can make' (p. 137). Clarke and Stewart (1988) offer a similar line of argument: 'Local government has always been and is a "people" business. Perhaps now, more than ever, it is recognised that the "people" resource needs to be managed and nurtured to give of its best ... All managers need to recognise their responsibilities for making sure the most is made of their staff' (p. 20).

What this emphasises is the need for an enlightened form of management – enlightened in the sense of being aware of, and responsive to, the various ways in which an organisation can do harm to its staff. As Pottage and Evans (1992) emphasise, we must try to move away from traditional 'macho' notions of 'be tough' as these only serve to reinforce an oppressive and destructive organisational culture. This involves seeing staff care as an integral part of how social work agencies are run, rather than a luxury item to be acquired if finances permit. Coulshed (1990) makes a similar point: 'Women colleagues tell me that they have been trying to persuade their managers to see that concern for people's needs at work and honest relationships are signs of strength, not weakness' (p. 5).

A short-sighted approach which sees staff care as a cost rather than an investment is one which leaves staff vulnerable and unsupported – it is a risky strategy and a potential recipe for disaster. This is a point to which we shall return in Chapter 7.

Whilst emphasising the need for a more enlightened approach to management, we should not lose sight of the role practitioners can play in dealing with the extrinsic organisational stressors we have outlined in this chapter. It is not simply a matter of arguing for a better managerial response. There are two ways in which staff can contribute to a more positive approach to the organisational dimension of stress. First, we can ensure, as far as possible, that our own responses to the situation are geared towards minimising the pressures. The subjective dimension of our response to pressures is an important one. Frankl (1973) captures this point in the following passage: 'Man is not free from conditions, be they biological or psychological or sociological in nature. But he is, and always remains, free to take a stand towards these conditions; he always retains the freedom to choose his attitude towards them' (p. 15). To Frankl's biological, psychological and sociological, we could add our own 'organisational' and the same point would still hold true. We retain the capacity to 'make the best of a bad job'.

Second, we need to ask what part we are playing in maintaining the management practices or agency culture that oppress us. One example of this is the question posed by

Morrison (1993) when he discusses the dynamics which sustain a culture in which supervision is marginalised or seen as a luxury that cannot be afforded. He asks practitioners to consider: 'What part do you play in colluding with not receiving supervision?' This is not a subtle form of 'blaming the victim', but rather a recognition of the complex and intricate processes which go on to allow unsatisfactory working practices to continue relatively unchallenged. We need to develop an awareness of what steps we can take, however small, to break down unhelpful organisational practices and structures. Organisational cultures are not fixed once and for all; they have to be recreated day by day and transmitted from one generation of workers to the next. Once again this produces a situation where there is no neutral middle ground – our actions and attitudes will either contribute to challenging the organisational framework and the stress problems it generates, or they will condone, and thus reinforce, that framework. This sets us the challenge of developing a greater awareness of our own organisational behaviour – part of the wider stress management strategy of heightened self-awareness, a point to which we shall return in Chapter 8.

The 1990s is a time of tremendous change in terms of how managers and organisations operate, linked to a dwindling faith in the appropriateness of traditional bureaucracy as an organising principle for managing large organisations. New philosophies demand new approaches to management. As Clarke and Stewart (1988) put it: 'Being close to the customer and citizen demands a capacity to learn, respond and adapt far removed from the traditional bureaucratic organisation designed for stability and continuity' (p. 11). This changing managerial and organisational context provides an excellent opportunity for promoting positive change and playing a part in developing organisations in which the notion that 'people matter' becomes more than a rhetorical slogan.

7

Prevention and Remedy

There is no shortage of literature on the subject of stress which offers practical advice on how to avoid experiencing stress or, once stress is encountered, how to cope with its effects or come to terms with its aftermath. A major focus in this type of book is what could be called the 'health education' dimension of stress management. This concentrates on matters of diet, exercise and so on.

As has been suggested, these aspects *are* important, but it is probably fair to say that their significance has been overemphasised at the expense of other factors which have therefore had to take a back seat. This chapter seeks to go some way towards rectifying this situation by exploring a number of stress management issues which have hitherto been marginalised – particularly those which relate to the specific context of stress in social work.

The chapter is divided into four main sections. The first is concerned with managing *pressure*. It considers strategies for dealing with social work pressures in an attempt to ensure that they are manageable; that is, they are not allowed to spill over into stress. The emphasis is therefore on prevention.

The second part addresses issues of managing *stress*. It explores the strategies that can be used to deal with stress, the positive steps that can be taken to minimise or remedy the harmful effects of stress. It therefore relates to those situations where pressure has reached an inappropriate level and is harming the person or group concerned. Consequently, the emphasis is on harm reduction and re-establishing equilibrium.

The third part is concerned with managing the aftermath of a period of stress or a traumatic incident. It examines some of the difficulties involved in helping staff to 'pick up the pieces' and deal with the intense emotions which tend to be generated at such times. The emphasis is on the role of, and need for, adequate support and protection systems.

The fourth part presents an overview of the role of training in the management of pressure and stress. It examines how training can contribute to equipping practitioners to deal with the pressure they face. Furthermore, it explores the dual role training can play with regard to managers – relating to dealing with their own pressures *and* providing support for the staff for whom they have supervisory or managerial responsibility.

Managing pressure

Perhaps one of the most important aspects of managing pressure is a certain degree of self-awareness, a sensitivity to stressors and their effects. Pressures can easily build up gradually without our realising. We adjust steadily and gradually as pressures increase, and so it is not unusual for us to fail to appreciate the extent or nature of the pressures we face. This is a dangerous state of affairs as it means that we can leave ourselves vulnerable to stress, unprepared for any additional pressures – only one straw away from a 'last straw' situation. Self-awareness is therefore an important, if not essential, aspect of managing pressure. It involves maintaining an overview of the current demands being made of us. This is a key part of 'boundary-setting' a point to which we shall return below.

Practice Focus 7.1

Heather was the team leader of a large childcare team within a Social Services Department. She shared with the remainder of the team considerable concern about the changes occurring as a result of the implementation of a new piece of legislation. In particular, Heather was beginning to notice subtle negative changes in the team atmosphere, changes that she did not like or understand.

In response to this, Heather arranged an 'awayday'. She organised a full day away from the office so that they could address a number of issues, including team morale. During the course of the day it became apparent that the least powerful group of staff – the (female) social work assistants – had been put under considerable pressure directly as a result of increased workload in one particular aspect of their job. They had not felt able to bring this issue to a team meeting, thus increasing the pressure they experienced.

However, once the issue was brought out into the open, Heather was able to review priorities and reorganise workloads. Early intervention by the team leader had prevented severe pressure on one group of staff from resulting in health-affecting stress.

Maintaining an overview is a valuable skill in managing pressure. It is often referred to as 'helicopter vision' – the ability to rise above a situation, get a clear picture of what is happening and then descend back into the picture to deal with it. One useful way of doing this is to carry out a 'pressure audit'. This amounts to making a list (or drawing a diagram if you find this more helpful) of all the pressures to which you are subject at the present moment, and then ranking them in order of priority or significance. This tactic is likely to have two positive effects – even if the list of pressures is a long and daunting one:

1. It helps to get the situation in perspective. It begins to give a sense of control and order – important aspects of managing pressure. It can therefore act as a confidence booster.
2. By outlining the range of pressures and their relative importance, the 'pressure audit' sets the scene for

developing a plan of action. It gives us a 'map' of our pressures and therefore enables us to make a start on plotting a route through them – or, better still, plotting a number of routes and evaluating which is the best one to pursue.

Self-awareness will not, in itself, keep pressures within manageable limits, but it none the less has an important part to play. It is a necessary condition but not a sufficient one. It is also a basic pre-condition for another important aspect of managing pressure, that of assertiveness.

Being assertive involves achieving a balance between the two extremes of submission and aggression. It entails achieving a degree of harmony in our dealings with others by seeking a 'win-win' situation – one in which we are able to achieve an agreement so that both parties can get what they want, but not at the other's expense. Assertiveness is an approach to conflict management which can help avoid the pressure arising from aggression – whether as victim or perpetrator. As Cousins (1991) comments: 'An assertive person respects him or herself and those they deal with. They recognise and accept their own positive and negative qualities and in doing so are able to be more authentic in their acceptance of others. They do not need to put others down in order to feel good themselves' (p. 23).

Assertiveness is therefore an important aspect of managing pressure and one which social work staff would do well to develop (see, for example, Back and Back, 1982). In particular, this approach has much to offer women for, as Cousins notes:

Social workers often find it hard to set limits on the amount of time and attention they give to others. They feel guilty if they think they are failing to meet other people's needs, yet they often find it impossible to say no and equally impossible to make their own needs and feelings known . . . Significantly, women outnumber men in this work and it is traditionally women who have been socialised to gain approval through putting the needs and expectations of others before their own (Cousins, 1991, p. 23).

The ability to say 'no' is a matter of boundary-setting and this involves being clear about what extent and type of pressure we are able and willing to accept. Assertiveness is the process by which we communicate those boundaries to others, clearly, constructively and in a spirit of mutual respect.

Boundary-setting is also an issue with regard to responsibility. In social work levels of personal responsibility tend to be very high. However, there is a danger that staff can find themselves feeling responsible for matters over which they have little or no control. This is a very significant danger as responsibility without control is potentially a recipe for disaster. Managing pressure therefore involves being clear about where our responsibilities begin and end. For example, resource shortfall may mean that staff are not able to meet identified need. In such cases we must be careful not to take this as personal failure and feel guilty.

Staff new to social work often find this especially difficult – having to accept that so many problems are beyond our control and solutions are out of reach. This further emphasises the need for clarity concerning individual responsibility, team or staff group responsibility and agency or wider society responsibility. Figure 7.1 captures these overlapping, but none the less distinct, levels of responsibility.

Boundary-setting also applies to another key element of managing pressure, that of time management. Time pressures can play a significant part in the development of pressure into stress and so it pay dividends to devote some time and attention to developing time management skills and techniques. Even some simple and basic steps in this direction can have major benefits in terms of keeping pressures under control:

- Use your diary systematically and consistently to keep track of commitments by drawing a line down the middle of the page; the left hand column can be used to note down appointments, meetings and so on while the right hand side can be where you list tasks to complete, people to telephone, letters to write and so on.
- At the beginning of each working day, review what tasks you have to complete that day and rank them in priority

Figure 7.1 *Boundaries of responsibility*

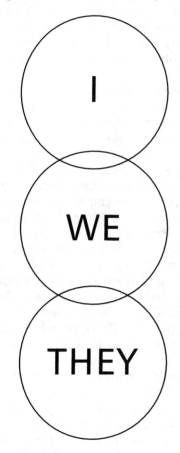

Source: Based on training materials prepared by Tony Morrison.

order. Note any that you do not relish doing and, if possible, do them first. Putting them off will slow you down and get in the way of progress, whereas getting them out of the way will make a positive start to the day.

- Try not to get bogged down with a multitude of small tasks. If a small problem can be solved there and then when it arises, beware of putting it off until later just because it is not of major significance. Minor problems not dealt with quickly can easily become major problems. Also, sorting these out quickly is a good confidence boost and source of motivation – nothing succeeds like success.

Time management is perhaps a misnomer as the fundamental element underpinning all this is the management of energy and motivation. Once again, it is a matter of taking control of our lives, putting ourselves in the driving seat and thereby not letting pressures get on top of us.

We were earlier critical of the many books that adopt a simplistic health education approach to matters of stress. However, it is important to emphasise that it is their narrow over-reliance on such matters which is problematic rather than their relevance to this field of study. Questions of smoking, alcohol consumption, diet and exercise are all very significant with regard to managing pressure and avoiding stress. However, as they have been more than adequately covered elsewhere, we shall not dwell on them here except to emphasise that failing to take account of these issues is a dangerous strategy, the effects of which could so easily undermine progress made in other areas of managing pressure.

Diet, exercise and so on are also relevant with regard to the range of coping methods we use. As we have seen, coping responses can be either positive and constructive or negative and destructive. Sporting exercise or alcohol in moderation would be examples of positive coping methods while abandoning a sensible diet (whether by not eating or overeating) or abusing alcohol would be negative and potentially harmful.

Understanding our own characteristic coping responses is an important, if not essential, part of managing pressure. There is much to be gained from identifying our positive methods, consolidating them and, where possible, adding to our repertoire. Similarly, identifying our negative methods and trying to resist relying upon them is a good way of reducing our vulnerability to stress. It is worthwhile drawing up such lists of positives and negatives (an exercise similar to the 'pressure audit' mentioned above) as part of developing a systematic and reliable approach to managing pressure.

In addition to these important steps that we can take to modify and strengthen our management of pressure, we must also take account of the dimension so often paid scant attention, that of support. Support is a vague and indeterminate term but a highly pertinent one none the less. It can take a number of forms, as Figure 7.2 illustrates, and each of these has much to offer as in our efforts to manage the pressures we face in social work, and in our lives in general.

Figure 7.2 *Typology of support*

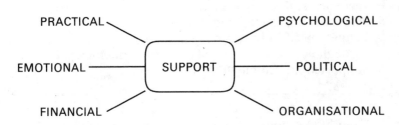

Perhaps the two most important messages we can give with regard to support are:

1. Take stock of what sources of support are available to you – formal and informal, both in the work sphere and beyond – and do not be afraid to draw on that support as and when you need it. Using support – and providing it, too – are important parts of the process of breaking down 'be tough' attitudes and creating a 'culture of permission', an ethos which allows people to acknowledge their vulnerability and their need to be supported;
2. Identify gaps and inadequacies in your support network and consider what steps can be taken to fill them. Managing pressure is about being proactive and this involves using the supports available to us whilst also laying the foundations for rectifying any shortfall

identified. In keeping with the spirit of mutual support, this is perhaps best done collectively in team or staff group meetings rather than as an individual undertaking.

Practice Focus 7.2

Ceris was returning to the office after a long and particularly difficult assessment visit to a client with mental health problems. It was 6.30 pm and Ceris felt quite drained. The client had threatened violence, his family had been very upset and she felt tired and very isolated. As she let herself into the office, she noticed there was still someone in her team room. She discovered that two colleagues and her team leader had stayed behind specifically to give her the opportunity to talk through her difficult visit. She cried, feeling looked after, supported and so much better.

Focusing on support is, of course, not a sign of weakness or an admission of defeat or failure. It is a recognition that social work is a pressurised activity and staff who seek to manage these pressures without support are running unnecessary risks and, moreover, are contributing to the destructive 'macho' culture which promotes 'the attitude among social care staff that to acknowledge the experience of occupational stress is a personal and professional failure' (McDerment, 1992, p. 13). Indeed, as McDerment goes on to comment: 'We will never tackle the issue of dysfunctional stress in the caring field unless we address this arrogant attitude' (1992, p. 13).

Coping with stress

On those occasions when pressure overspills into stress, support also has a significant bearing on how constructively the situation is handled. Experiencing stress means that our pressure management techniques have been overwhelmed; we have reached a stage where the pressure is such that we experience it as harmful, a threat to our health and well-being. At such times support takes on even greater significance; it can, in fact, become crucial, a critical variable in determining the length and intensity of stress experienced.

This makes the creation of a 'culture of permission' all the more important. In work situations where staff feel able to admit feeling stressed without fear of being judged or blamed, the prospects for minimising the negative effects of such stress are greatly increased. A supportive ethos prevents the need for bottling up feelings or allowing frustrations and tensions to fester and weaken us. Very often the simple recognition of stress is enough to mobilise support – and this mobilisation of support can, in turn, give us so much reassurance, strength and confidence that the stress very quickly recedes back into manageable pressure. Remember that stress is our *response* to an inappropriate level of pressure. Being reminded or reassured that support is available can be very powerful in making that response a more positive one.

But, before we can call upon support, we need to recognise our own stress, to be aware of how our pressures are getting on top of us or are hurting us. Stress, like depression, is something which can affect us without our realising. Due to the nature of stress we can become so preoccupied with our pressures that we do not notice the harm they are causing; we do not appreciate just what is happening to us. For this reason, it is often those around us who bring stress to our attention, who raise concern about our well-being.

Whether we recognise the stress for ourselves or need to have it pointed out to us, we would, none the less, be wise to try to respond quickly to take the necessary steps before the situation gets worse. The reason for this is that stress tends to be cyclical (Thompson, 1991a) – stress begets stress, and we find ourselves getting deeper and deeper into a hole. The central task, therefore, is to break out of the cyclical pattern and re-establish equilibrium.

Clearly, mobilising support systems is a key part of this process. An important aspect of coping with stress, therefore, is being able to acknowledge that we are under stress and that we need help. Often, however, (misguided) feelings of guilt or inadequacy can act as a significant barrier to this. None the less, we can only begin to deal with stress when we take this significant step forward and accept that we are under stress.

Sometimes there will be no immediate objective resolution of the stress-generating situation as, for example, at times of staff shortage. However, the situation can be eased by setting personal and team boundaries and accepting the limitations of what can be achieved in the circumstances. Referring back to Figure 7.1, we need to ensure that we are not carrying on our shoulders a burden that belongs elsewhere. Social work staff cannot be held responsible for the service shortfall created by resource restrictions and those staff who take this on board personally and feel they are failing are, in effect, putting themselves in a no-win situation. Political problems require political solutions and, whilst staff, both individually and collectively, can contribute to the political process, this is not to say that they can be held to account for the failings of the wider system. Social work staff are already vulnerable to being scapegoated for structural and systems weaknesses without volunteering for the job. Reviewing boundaries and, if necessary realigning them, is therefore a valuable part of coping with stress and re-establishing control.

This type of review or realignment is an example of a 'survival strategy', one which comes under the general heading of 'reframing' or 'cognitive restructuring'. It amounts to seeing the situation in a new light or from a new perspective. This reflects the fact that stress is a phenomenon which operates at the intersection of objective and subjective factors. Even in situations where there is little that we can do to alter the objective stressors, we can often achieve a great deal by altering our *attitude* towards those stressors. For example, adopting an attitude of calm confidence can be instrumental in reducing the impact of stressors and returning to a situation where pressures are experienced as manageable. Many of these necessary changes – reviewing boundaries, avoiding inappropriate shouldering of responsibility, achieving renewed confidence – can, and *should* flow quite spontaneously from good quality supervision. Staff who are experiencing stress without being able to rely on skilled and effective supervision are in an unnecessarily vulnerable position. There is a long-standing tradition of staff supervision in fieldwork and increasingly this pattern is becoming established in residential work. Staff should expect at least a basic standard of supportive supervision and, where this is not forthcoming from official sources, should at least attempt to get such supervisory support from other, perhaps more informal, sources.

Practice Focus 7.3

Joseph was a residential worker in a home for older people. He was a very mild, pleasant and tactful worker. One evening, the officer-in-charge found him speaking to the relatives of a very sick resident in a raised voice, virtually shouting at them.

In supervision the next day his manager attempted to discover what was going on. Joseph explained that these particular relatives 'got on his nerves' and he could barely control his frustration with them. His supervisor suggested he see the counsellor. Initially Joseph refused but later agreed to attend for one session. In fact, he attended for a total of five sessions during which he worked on his feelings around the death of his mother some five years earlier and the subsequent relationships with the other members of his family.

Counselling had prevented the need for Joseph to take sick leave and he declared that he had not felt so good for years. His colleagues and the residents were delighted to see the positive changes in him.

A further reason for emphasising the importance of supervision is that people under stress can have a tendency to be very harsh on themselves, to indulge in self-blame and self-deprecation. This is perhaps a matter of self-esteem as stress can have a very detrimental effect on our sense of self-worth. Stress can lead us to be very hard on ourselves, often much harder than we would be on other people in the same circumstances. A good supervisor can recognise that this process is going on and take steps to help get the situation back in perspective and in proportion.

At times of stress we need to resist this temptation to be hard on ourselves and, if anything, we should go to the other extreme and take whatever opportunities we can to feel good about ourselves. This is likely to involve finding some personal space, giving ourselves a special treat or two, spending some time with the people we love and so on – in short, anything which can, in some way counterbalance the negative and harmful effects of the stress. We should not feel guilty for having personal needs – for relaxation, pleasure, affection and positive strokes. Martyrdom has no place in social work.

Time out is one way of achieving this. Getting some distance between ourselves and the pressures we face is a very constructive way of coping with our pressures especially when they are of such magnitude that they are experienced as stressful. This is not a form of escapism, but rather a helpful way of 'recharging our batteries'. The more enlightened employers, those that take the notion of human resource management seriously, already have in place schemes for giving staff time out following periods when they have had to face unrealistically high levels or pressure.

Perhaps the most important component of coping with stress, notwithstanding the crucial role of support already mentioned, is the development of a positive outlook. Digging ourselves out of the pit of stress involves a degree of confidence, determination and a positive belief that things can be better, that life does not have to be so painful. Once again supervision has a part to play here, a key role in instilling a positive and constructive approach. A good supervisor is an invaluable ally in ensuring that hope does not succumb to the powerful and insistent pull of despair. Without hope, burnout and a chronically negative outlook are never far away.

Aftermath and recovery

With short periods of stress the question of recovery barely arises as we are so often able to slip in and out of periods of stress without making any major adjustments. However, there are occasions when a period of stress has been so prolonged or so intense that returning to a state of equilibrium is a difficult and perhaps lengthy process. This especially applies when staff are subject to particularly traumatic incidents, such as a physical assault or a serious threat or abuse.

At such times it is important that steps are taken to facilitate recovery so that the trauma does not leave a permanent scar. As Pynoos and Eth (1984) comment: 'Trauma occurs when an individual is exposed to an overwhelming event that renders him or her helpless in the face of intolerable danger, anxiety and instinctual arousal' (quoted by Judd, 1992). However, one problem with this comment is that it implies that trauma relates to a specific event whereas, in the sense that we are using it here, it is also applicable to the situations which arise from extended periods of stress. It is not only *in*tensive stressors (specific incidents) that can prove traumatic but also *ex*tensive stressors (chronic staff shortages, for example) – see Scott and Stradling (1992, 1993).

An important part of recovering from trauma is to have the opportunity for 'debriefing', as the literature on posttraumatic stress confirms (for example, Scott and Stradling, 1992). Debriefing involves discussing the situation with a colleague, manager or counsellor, focusing on the emotional impact of the circumstances and thus providing a significant source of personal support.

Practice Focus 7.4

It was a complicated child protection case. Four members of the team had been involved over a period of four years. They had gradually and reluctantly come to the conclusion that care proceedings and permanent separation were necessary for the well-being of the children concerned.

They prepared the case for court. However, on the day of the hearing, the judge was hostile and rejected the application. The attitude of the parents' barrister was vindictive, even vitriolic. The workers left the court feeling exhausted, devalued, chastised and totally lacking in self-esteem.

The team leader recognised the difficulties the workers had experienced and the destructive potential of the situation. He therefore arranged for an experienced colleague to act as a facilitator to the team and help them recover from this very distressing incident. This was achieved by a mixture of 'ventilation' and cognitive restructuring techniques and proved to be a very successful means of dealing with the aftermath.

We must be careful, though, to distinguish between post-traumatic incidents or prolonged periods of duress – and the much more serious condition of post-traumatic stress *disorder* (PTSD):

Raphael (1990) warns that post-traumatic reactions should not be equated with post-traumatic stress disorder (PTSD). Hysteria, confusional states and even brief psychoses are known to occur in the short-term but quickly clear up. They are transitional states and are not therefore signs of a deep psychological disorder. It is only when such problems persist over time that the term PTSD becomes applicable (Thompson, 1991b, p. 93).

What is particularly important about maintaining this distinction is that a failure to do so increases the risk of 'blaming the victim' by applying an individualised clinical label to what is, after all, a wider organisational matter. That is, misapplying the label 'PTSD' can have the potential effect of reinforcing a sense of guilt and personal responsibility for the circumstances leading to the trauma. Indeed, a primary function of debriefing is to discourage and undermine the common tendency of staff to see the situation as a consequence of their own mistakes or inadequacies.

Breakwell (1989) relates this specifically to feelings of guilt which arise in the aftermath of a particular type of trauma, that of physical assault: 'The assaulted often think that it is some failing in their professional skills which has made them incapable of defusing the violent situation and preventing the attack' (p. 75). She then goes on to generalise from this:

> The guilt response is common in many traumatically stressful incidents. For instance, survivors of tragedy where others die often feel guilt despite being innocent of any responsibility for the disaster. The guilt of victims may be a symptom of stress rather than any rational evaluation of responsibility for the event. Guilt is a debilitating response. It often leads to self-doubt and blame. These in turn destroy confidence and authority. Work becomes a nightmare (1989, p. 75).

Efforts geared towards helping people cope with the aftermath of trauma therefore need to be sensitive to this proneness to guilt and self-blame. This entails staff who experience such trauma needing to resist such feelings of guilt and, perhaps more realistically, it entails staff who are cast in a supportive role doing all that they can to avoid such feelings being reinforced.

Attempting to remove this sense of guilt and failure is a key part of debriefing and, if necessary, longer-term counselling. Such supportive intervention may be required to help repair the damage done to self-esteem by prolonged or intense distress. However, the question of stress counselling is one that needs to be handled carefully.

As we noted earlier, Murphy (1991) found that staff were reluctant to accept offers of counselling help as they recognised that the problem lay not within them, but within the wider circumstances of the situation in which they found themselves. There are, of course, additional reasons why counselling is not a popular option:

- there are concerns that accepting counselling will be an acceptance of failure, or a recognition that the problem is one of our own fault or inadequacy
- suspicions may be raised that counselling will be linked to appraisal; that is, it may act as a barrier to career progression and job security

These are both examples of 'blaming the victim'; that is, they both reduce a complex organisational social and psychological matter to a simple example of individual weakness or failing. They reflect a reductionist 'pathological' approach – one which, although theoretically inadequate, is, unfortunately, a none the less commonplace one. Ironically, one of the primary tasks of counselling is to move away from this tendency to blame the victim and help transcend feelings of guilt, failure or inadequacy.

The experience of trauma can leave staff struggling to find or reconstruct a thread of meaning or sense of purpose and direction in their lives. Counselling can therefore play a major part in helping to overcome this problem. A variety of techniques are available, including as Totman (1990) points out, a range of 'attribution therapies':

> Attribution therapists use various techniques to replace attitudes of helplessness and negativity with attitudes of effectiveness – in particular the attitude that one has control over one's life. This is referred to by various names, 'personal control training', 'assertiveness training', 'social skills training', 'cognitive restructuring', and so forth. The essence of these therapies is that someone (the therapist) injects meaning into someone else's (the client's) life using professional techniques to change attitudes about the self (p.174).

The potential value of counselling is immense, provided that the barriers to its usage can be removed. That is, it must be made clear that it is

- fully confidential
- not linked to appraisal
- not seen as an acknowledgement of personal weakness, error or inadequacy

We would suggest that this is unlikely to be achieved unless counselling is offered as part of a wider staff care policy, that is, a reflection, and integral part, of an organisational commitment to supporting staff through the difficulties, demands and painful experiences inherent in an occupation as challenging as social work.

The aftermath of intense or extended stress is usually a difficult period of adjustment in which the support of others can, and so often does, play a major role in determining the speed, effectiveness and personal cost of that adjustment. However, whilst offers of support in the aftermath of a specific trauma are usually forthcoming, there are other such situations where support is often withheld or not thought necessary. These are the situations in which staff experience what has become known as 'burnout'.

The sort of aftermath we have discussed so far is characterised by a recognition and acceptance of the stress factors and their impact. However, for many staff, the effects of long-term stress are less visible and more insidious in their influence. Burnout tends to arise not after a specific incident or a clearly defined period of duress (for example, a period of staff shortage) but, rather, as a result of a lengthier process of gradual disillusionment and disenchantment. The result is broadly the same as a more overtly traumatic experience of stress – a loss of purpose, meaning and direction. Burnard (1991) uses the term 'dispiritedness' to describe such scenarios:

> Perhaps the most stressful situation of all is the fact of having an inability to find meaning at all. Such a state may be described as *dispiritedness*. Dispiritedness then, is the fact of being unable to invest life with meaning. It is sometimes, but not always, combined with depression. When it is not, it is characterized by a general sense of loss, a lack of conviction in what one is doing and a lack of enthusiasm for life in general. It may also be accompanied by a sense of cynicism and by the development of 'gallows humour' (p. 87).

Burnout can be seen to be characterised by such dispiritedness. Workers lose commitment and enthusiasm to the point where they cannot deal with pain or distress on the part of clients. They therefore become cold, distant and cynical, anaesthetised from their own and others' pain. This makes burnout a very difficult situation to deal with. The nature of the condition makes it unlikely that those affected will be motivated to seek help or accept it if it is offered. Burnout is a form of emotional exhaustion which leaves the worker feeling alienated and powerlessness. It can be linked with what Pottage and Evans (1992) call 'pervasive stress':

> Pervasive stress . . . derives from an individual's experience of the organisation over long periods. The event or the point in time when a problem becomes acknowledged by the individual or by those around them may not have a clear cause/effect relationship, and be no more than a trigger which brings the underlying problem into the open (p. 25).

Such pervasive stress, when it manifests itself as burnout, tends to lead to a high level of inertia and a low level of motivation. Consequently, strategies for coping with this type of aftermath face an uphill struggle. There can be no simple or generalised solutions. Each situation must be taken on its merits.

The difficulties involved in recovering from intense or extended stress serve to emphasise the point made earlier, namely the major importance of preventing pressure from overspilling into stress in the first place. The costs, personal, financial and organisational, of 'picking up the pieces' far exceed those of preventing stress and trauma. As Morrison (1990) puts it: 'What is required is a preventative approach – we must change the environment in which people work rather than rescue them from it' (p. 265).

Training

We noted in Chapter 6 that training and development can be instrumental in helping staff manage pressures and avoid stress. Training is an essential component of human resource management, a key part of a 'healthy' organisation. All training and development activities are therefore important cogs in the machinery of stress management. However, our focus here is more specific and centres on training related more directly to the knowledge, skills and attitudes necessary for effective stress management. We begin by examining 'self-protection' training, geared towards dealing with our own pressures. We shall then move on to consider the training needs of managers and supervisors, training geared toward protecting and supporting others.

The traditional focus in stress management training could be described as a 'health education' approach with a heavy emphasis on diet, exercise and relaxation. As we have commented earlier, these aspects *are* important. However, they need to be seen in perspective – they form only a small part of the overall picture. There are many other important aspects that training can usefully address. These include:

- *Identifying stressors*. Training courses give a good opportunity for participants to gain an overview of the pressures they face. This is the beginning of gaining control.
- *Establishing coping resources*. Strategies for coping can be identified and distinctions drawn between those which are positive and constructive and those which are potentially problematic.
- *Mobilising support*. Participants can take the opportunity to map out their support networks, both formal and informal, and identify gaps and areas for consolidation This can give reassurances about strengths and warning about weaknesses or shortfall.

Exercises designed to cover these areas can help to paint a more holistic picture of stress than the traditional 'blame the victim' model which sees stress as a matter of individual failing. Indeed, we would argue that a central aim of training should be to dispel the myth that stress is the result of personal inadequacy or 'not being cut out for the job'. In addition to getting this essential message across, stress management training can allow participants to:

- develop their understanding of how stress can be managed and/or prevented

- identify and practise the skills (for example, self-management skills) involved in dealing effectively with stress
- increase confidence in managing pressure and stress and in identifying and (collectively) challenging organisational stressors and barriers to job satisfaction

In short, stress management training can succeed in raising consciousness of the issues and begin to empower staff to deal with them. An organisation, by providing such training for its staff, can thereby give a positive message of support and commitment to staff care.

Both of these matters – consciousness-raising and empowerment – are doubly important for managers and supervisors. This is because they have responsibility for stress management at two levels:

1. Managing their own pressures.
2. Helping to manage the pressures that impinge on the staff for whom they have managerial or supervisory responsibility.

That is, they are responsible not only for caring for themselves but also for promoting staff care. This involves developing or enhancing a range of good management practices which serve to protect staff and create a positive and supportive atmosphere where staff care is based more in reality than in rhetoric.

Training for managers and supervisors therefore needs to incorporate the elements of self-protection or 'self-care' as well as the additional elements of staff care. Consequently such training needs to include:

- developing an awareness of how management practices play a crucial role in exacerbating or reducing the pressures to which their staff are subject
- enhancing awareness of the factors that can render staff vulnerable to stress and/or burnout
- recognising the 'signs' that staff are experiencing stress or are in need of additional support

- understanding the importance of staff care policies and practice and underlining the need for a genuine commitment to making progress in these matters

Once again, such training is geared towards developing a more holistic view of stress and stress management. Managers and supervisors play a key role in creating an 'ethos of permission', an atmosphere in which staff feel able to talk openly about their pressures and stresses, their anxieties and fears, their pain. Sensitivity on the part of managers and supervisors is instrumental in creating the right type of working environment. For example, Cade (1983) comments that:

Supervisors should be trained to become more sensitive to the early signs of burn-out in their staff and be ready to counsel and advise or even order a worker under particular stress to take a break. It is important that burn-out not be seen as a 'personal failing' such that workers may hesitate to admit to such feelings (p. 10).

Social work organisations wishing to promote a genuine ethos of staff care therefore need to pay serious attention to providing a systematic programme of training not only for their practitioners but also for their supervisors and managers – indeed for all staff who contribute to the pressurised and often painful enterprise of dealing with deprivation and despair, problems and pain. To expect staff to undertake such tasks without adequate preparation and support is to take a firm and clear step in the direction of setting them up to fail.

Conclusion

Throughout this book we have attempted to merge theory with practice; that is, we have sought to draw on theoretical and research-based insights, not for their own sake, but rather as a guide to practice, a practical resource for dealing with stress. This chapter has been, in some ways, a culmination of that process, an attempt to distil the knowledge base built upon earlier chapters and deduce from this a set of strategies for stress management. It has sought to bring these issues together into a coherent approach to dealing with stress.

By focusing on the three 'stages' of dealing with stress – managing pressure, coping with stress and recovering from stress or trauma – we have offered practical guidance in relation to the different strategies that are required and, in the process, have highlighted some of the complexities and dilemmas that arise. What remains for us to do is to sketch out, in summary form, the lessons learned from each of the chapters and spell out the conclusions that can be drawn. This is precisely the task of the final chapter and it is to this that we now turn.

8

Conclusion

One thing this book has, we hope, made clear is that dealing with stress is not a simple or straightforward matter. The issues are subtle and intricate, the demands upon us complex and often intense. One implication of this is that there is a very strong need for clear and relatively simple guidance as to how to deal with these matters. This chapter, then, plays a dual role. On the one hand, it acts as a traditional final chapter with a focus on summarising the main issues and drawing the book to a logical close. On the other hand, however, it is also intended as a guide and reference point, a resource to assist social work staff in rising to the stress challenge. As a consequence of this dual role, the exposition is something of a hybrid, involving a mixture of conventional text and a range of charts and diagrams to act as a practical guide.

We therefore hope that this chapter will not only act as a useful summary but also as a practical resource for future learning and development. In short, we see it not only as an ending but also as a beginning. We shall revisit, in turn, each of the preceding seven chapters and attempt to distil from them the main points and issues, and the lessons we can learn from having an increased awareness of these matters.

Chapter 1 set the scene by reviewing the costs of stress, the variety of ways in which stress causes harm – whether to individuals, to teams or staff groups, or to whole organisations. Fundamental to this discussion was the distinction between pressure and stress. Whilst pressure is neutral – it can be positive or negative – stress is always negative. Stress arises when we respond to an inappropriate level of pressure. The level can be inappropriate because it is too low and leaves us feeling understimulated and demotivated. However, what occurs much more frequently is a level which is inappropriate because it is too high. Demand on our energies exceeds what our coping resources can supply. Like a physical structure exposed to too much pressure, we show signs of strain and, if the pressure does not decrease or if adequate support is not offered, the whole structure can collapse. Stress is therefore a very costly entity, insidious in its effects and potentially disastrous in its overall impact. Chapter 1 therefore laid heavy emphasis on the harm that stress can do, the costs it can incur in personal, social, financial, organisational and professional terms.

The personal costs are many and varied and, to a certain extent, specific to the individual(s) concerned. However, there are certain patterns or common threads that can be discerned, as summarised in Figure 8.1.

Figure 8.1   *The personal costs of stress*

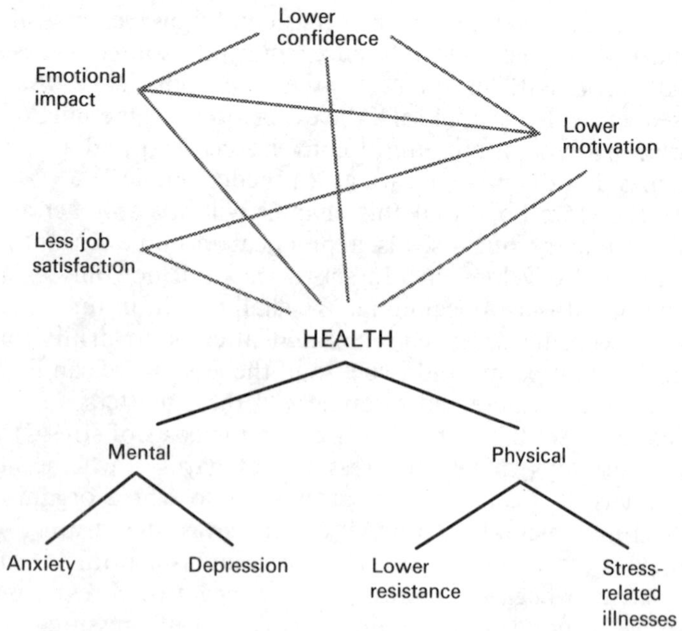

In addition, there are wider social costs above and beyond those experienced by the individual. These include: tension and ill-feeling within staff groups, strained relationships and a negative, cynical and demoralised work atmosphere. Once staff groups reach this point, the costs to the organisation can be of significant proportions, creating low morale, reduced productivity, high sickness rates and so on. Such organisations are then more likely to increase the professional costs of stress – poor standards of practice, a lower level of service and an increased risk of error.

Chapter 2 introduced a three-factor model of stress in preference to the traditional two-factor 'push–pull' model which encompasses the 'push' of stressors and the 'pull' of coping methods, but pays little or no attention to the crucial role of support systems. The main problem with the two-factor model is that it 'pathologises' the stress victim by presenting him or her as being weak or inadequate. This simplistic model sees stress as a mathematical equation: if pressure exceeds coping strength, stress will be experienced. If coping strength is greater than the amount or level of pressure, stress will not be experienced. By failing to take account of the role of support, this traditional model disregards the context in which pressures arise and in which coping takes place. What is needed, therefore, is a *three*-factor model which incorporates issues of support – and the impact support can have by reducing pressures and enhancing coping methods (see Figure 8.2). Support is a key concept which locates pressure and coping within their social and organisational context.

Chapter 2 also focused on sources of pressure or, to use the technical term, 'stressors'. These come in many shapes and sizes and vary considerably from setting to setting. However, we were able to identify certain common theories or recurring patterns. These are summarised in Figure 8.3.

Chapter 3 explored some of the complex issues of stress, coping and personality. As stress has a significant subjective component, personality needs to be recognised as an important variable, a major influence on how pressures are experienced and how they are dealt with. Personality acts as a 'filter', the medium through which life experiences are interpreted and shaped. How we respond to our life pressures

Figure 8.2 *The three-factor model of stress*

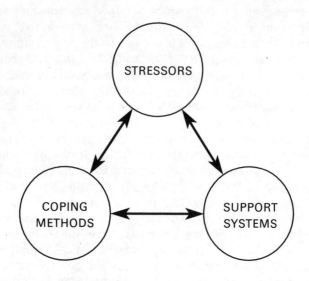

Figure 8.3 *Common stressors*

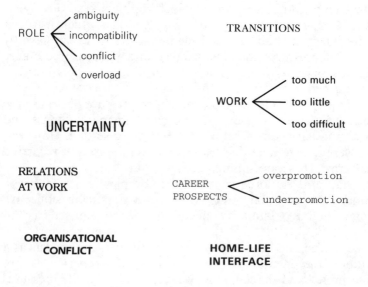

will therefore depend to a large extent, on our personality, our characteristic patterns of interacting with the world. A number of theories of personality were briefly explored: psychodynamics, behaviourism, social learning theory, humanistic psychology, trait theories and so on.

From this we were able to proceed to examining a range of commonly used coping strategies (see Figure 8.4). Having a broad repertoire of coping methods is a wise precaution against the danger of pressure overspilling into stress. The coping methods discussed were not presented as stock answers or formulae to follow but, rather, as indicative of the range of coping responses available. The task for each of us is to develop our own set of coping methods – ones that suit our own circumstances, pressures and personalities. What works for one person may not work for another; and what works for you in one situation may not work in another – hence the need for a broad repertoire and a sensitivity to what is likely to be useful in each context.

Figure 8.4 *Coping strategies*

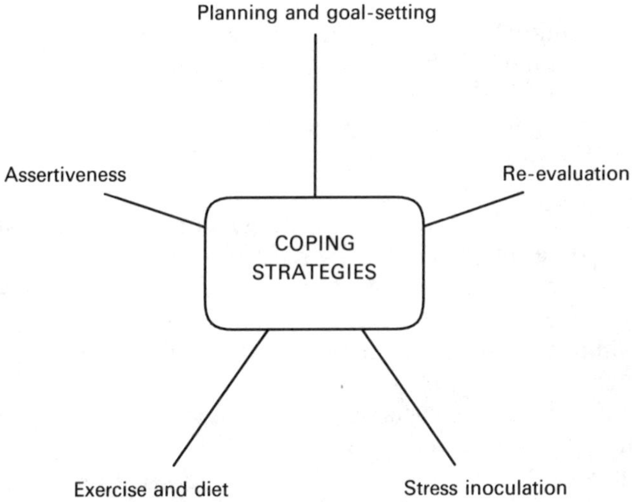

Planning and goal-setting

Assertiveness

Re-evaluation

COPING STRATEGIES

Exercise and diet

Stress inoculation

Whilst issues of personality and coping style have a central role in stress management, we also need to take account of the wider social context in which these occur. Chapter 4 tackled this task by focusing on the social divisions of race and gender. In particular, the additional pressures arising from sexism and racism were identified and the need for an anti-discriminatory approach was reaffirmed.

Black workers not only face racist comments and behaviour from clients but also have to contend with institutional racism within their organisations and even personal racism from their colleagues. Racism therefore brings with it extra pressures in addition to the other pressures social workers face. However, this is not all, as racism – through its insidious undermining of self esteem – can also have an adverse effect on coping abilities. The demoralisation and disempowerment of black workers by racism leaves such workers more vulnerable to stress.

There are also strong parallels between the effects of racism and those of sexism. The social division of gender and its associated forms of discrimination and oppression produce a situation in which women staff face additional pressures. These include:

- male domination, particularly in management
- sexist comments and/or actions on the part of clients and colleagues
- limited access to power, resources and promotion
- sexual harassment

As with racism, sexism not only generates extra pressures but also undermines coping by casting women in the role of 'natural' carers (and therefore resilient copers); by promoting feelings of guilt about wanting to have their needs met; by undermining self-esteem and encouraging an external locus of control.

Clearly, therefore, social divisions are an important part of our understanding of pressure and stress management. Attempts to deal with stress which pay no attention to social divisions can therefore be, at best, only partially successful. Chapter 4 focused specifically on issues of race and gender.

However, the point was also made that other social divisions as indicated in Figure 8.5 can also be very significant in terms of how pressures are experienced and managed.

Figure 8.5 *Social divisions*

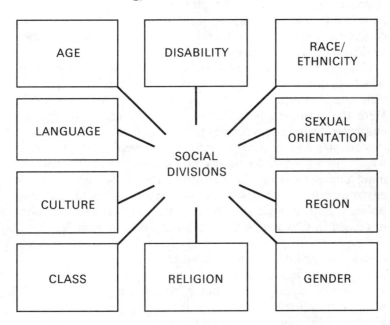

Chapter 5 also explored the broader context of stress, but this time specifically in relation to those factors that are intrinsic to the social work role – those problematic aspects of social work that can be improved or have their impact reduced but will never go away altogether. These include:

- the care versus control dilemma
- infinite demand balanced against finite supply
- being 'caught in the middle' between the interests of the state and the interests of the client
- dealing with vulnerability, pain and suffering

The underlying 'message' of Chapter 5 was one of acceptance, but not of resignation. Some problems cannot be resolved altogether and so we must learn to live with them. However, what is needed is not a spirit of passive resignation, but rather one of positive realism, geared towards coping as effectively as possible with the pressures. Without this positive approach we can easily fall victim of the destructive effects of frustration and hopelessness. Motivation and confidence suffer, leaving us more vulnerable to stress, less well-equipped to deal with the pressures we face.

Chapter 6 also dealt with issues relating to the context in which pressure and stress occur – but this time from a different perspective, that of the organisational framework. Here the approach needs to be very different, although the emphasis on being positive is no less applicable. The focus in this chapter was on those aspects of the organisational context which are amenable to change and improvement. That is, the main emphasis is on the *extrinsic* stressors within the work environment, those that are the result of organisational policies and practices, rather than the *intrinsic* stressors discussed in Chapter 5. The extrinsic stressors include:

- lack of facilities/poor working environment
- unsupportive management
- a lack of supervision, training, and so on
- a 'be tough' culture
- unrealistic workload expectations

Because these factors are amenable to change and improvement, an attitude of acceptance is likely to be counterproductive, leading to an ethos of compliance and resignation and thereby producing a spirit of defeatism. This, once again, would lead to feelings of hopelessness, low morale and low confidence and, therefore, increased susceptibility to stress. Once again, what is needed is an approach based on positive realism, a constructive attitude of cautious optimism. This involves striving for better working conditions, including a supportive culture and systems, but without becoming frustrated and demotivated when change does not come quickly enough.

Chapter 6 also had important implications for managers. Indeed, the role of manager or supervisor is a central one with regard to the management of pressure and stress. This is because managers have a responsibility for dealing with not only their own pressures but also those of the staff for whom they are responsible. It is for this reason that issues of stress management are doubly important for managers. People are increasingly being recognised as an organisation's most important resource. This being the case, managers have a crucial role in creating a supportive environment, promoting a positive culture and establishing staff care as reality rather than rhetoric.

Chapters 5 and 6 are inter-related in so far as they both go beyond the individual level of dealing with stress and pay attention to the wider issues of the nature of the social work role and the organisational context in which it is carried out. The two sets of issues (social work role and organisational context) combine to produce a complex picture but one which is helpful in mapping out the important interactions of the various elements. Figure 8.6 attempts to capture how these elements inter-relate.

Figure 8.6 *Contextual factors*

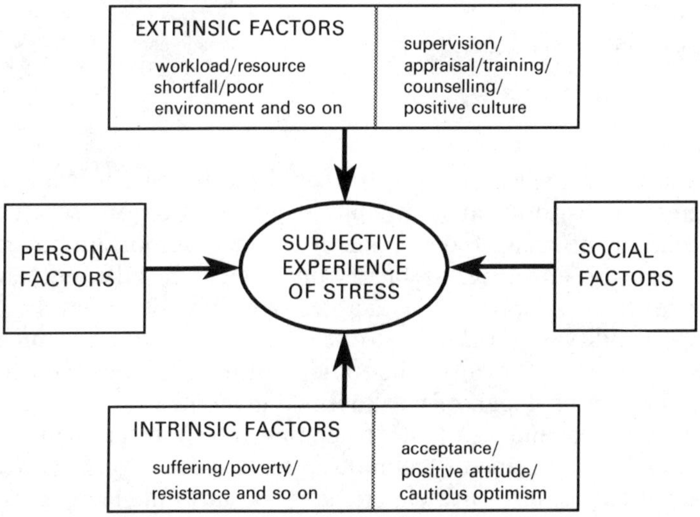

Chapter 7 has as its topic prevention and remedy. This was divided into four main parts; managing pressure, managing stress, managing the aftermath (of stress or trauma) and the significant role of training. In examining the management of pressure, the focus was on prevention – preventing pressure from overspilling into stress. We considered a range of strategies for keeping our work and life pressures within manageable limits, as Figure 8.7 illustrates.

Figure 8.7   *Managing pressure*

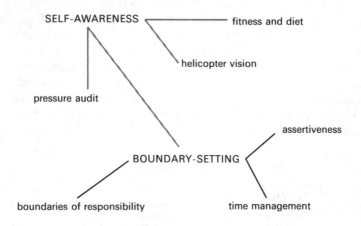

These strategies, though, are unlikely to be sufficient in themselves without at least some degree of support, whether formal or informal. Indeed, one of the most important coping strategies is ensuring, as far as possible, that sufficient and appropriate support is available. We have two levels of responsibility: *individually*, to seek out support and *collectively*, to break down the 'be tough' culture that sees the need for support as a sign of weakness or inadequacy.

The management of stress comes into effect when our pressure management techniques have been overwhelmed, when the pressures are experienced as harmful. Here again,

support has an important part to play, as indeed do the
following:

- acknowledging that we are under stress
- avoiding feelings of guilt or inadequacy
- reframing the situation in a more positive way
- resisting the temptation to be hard on ourselves

Coping with stress is about re-establishing control and
equilibrium and, in so doing, returning to a situation in which
pressures are manageable – and perceived as such. When this
takes a long time, for example, when the period of stress is
prolonged or particularly traumatic, then additional measures
for 'dealing with the aftermath' are likely to be necessary.
These measures include debriefing (the opportunity to talk
things through) and access to confidential independent
counselling.

All these attempts to deal with stress, whether preventative
or 'after the event', can be enhanced by training, by managers
and practitioners addressing the principles of stress management within a staff development framework. Chapter 7
explored some of the ways in which training courses on
dealing with stress can serve to equip the individual for the
demands of social work and, on a more collective basis,
contribute to creating a positive and supportive culture. The
two 'sides' of stress management training were discussed;
dealing with one's own pressures and supporting others in
dealing with theirs as part of a movement towards making
staff care a reality.

Thus, the focus of Chapter 7 was on applying theory to
practice, drawing out the practical implications of the various
issues discussed in earlier chapters. Indeed, this is a major aim
of the book overall – to develop a pragmatic approach to
stress management but one which is, none the less, grounded
in relevant theory and research. The task is not simply to
understand stress but to be able to use our increased
understanding to equip us to deal with pressure and stress
more effectively.

There can be no guarantees that we will not fall foul of
stress, that our pressures will not overwhelm us. But, what we

hope this book has made clear, is that there are steps that can be taken to minimise the likelihood of this happening; to help us recover quickly and satisfactorily if it does happen; and to deal sensitively and constructively with the subsequent aftermath. There are no guarantees, no simple formulae to follow, although, as we have seen, there is much that can be done to make social work a less stressful occupation. We hope that this book will help you in this difficult task and play at least a small part in equipping you to tackle your pressures positively, confidently and in a spirit of cautious optimism.

Bibliography

Adams, J. D. (1980) *Understanding and Managing Stress*, San Diego, University Associates.

Ahmad, B. (1990) *Black Perspectives in Social Work*, Birmingham, Venture Press.

Allan, M., Bhavnani, R. and French, K. (1992) *Promoting Women*, London, HMSO.

Andrisani, P. J. and Nestel, G. (1976) 'Internal-External Control as a Contributor to, and Outcome of Work Experience', *Journal of Applied Psychology*, 61.

Argyle, M. (1989) *The Social Psychology of Work*, Harmondsworth, Penguin.

Arnold, H. J. and Feldman, D. C. (1982) 'A Multi-Variant Analysis of the Determinants of Job Turnover', *Journal of Applied Psychology*, 67 (3).

Arroba, T. and James, K. (1987) *Pressure at Work: A Survival Guide*, London, McGraw-Hill.

Atkinson, R. L., Atkinson, R. C. and Hilgard, E. R. (1983) *Introduction to Psychology*, New York, Harcourt Brace Jovanovich.

Audit Commission (1985) *Good Management in Local Government*, London, HMSO.

Back, K. and Back, K. (1982) *Assertiveness at Work: A Practical Guide to Handling Awkward Situations*, London, McGraw-Hill.

Bandura, A. (1977) *A Social Learning Theory*, Englewood Cliffs, N.J., Prentice-Hall.

Barclay Committee, (1982) *Social Workers: Their Role and Tasks*, London, Bedford Square Press.

Barker, P. (1986) *Basic Family Therapy*, Oxford, Basil Blackwell.

Bate, P. (1992) 'The Impact of Organizational Culture on Approaches to Organizational Problem Solving', in Salaman (1992).

Berger, P. (1966) *Invitation to Sociology*, Harmondsworth, Penguin.

Berkowitz, A. D. and Perkins, H. W. (1984) 'Stress among Farm Women: Work and Family as Interacting Systems', *Journal of Marriage and Family*, 46.

Braike, H. B. (1986) 'The Stress of Success', *Working Woman*, August, 1986.

Bramhall, M. and Ezell, S. (1981) 'How Burned Out Are You?', *Public Welfare*, Winter, 1981.

Breakwell, G. (1989) *Facing Physical Violence*, London, Routledge.

Brown, A. (1984) *Consultation*, London, Heinemann.

167

Buck, V. (1972) *Working under Pressure*, London, Staples Press.

Burnard, P. (1991) *Coping with Stress in the Health Professions*, London, Chapman & Hall.

Burnout Study and Support Group (1986) 'Less Sympathy for Women', *Social Work Today*, 17.

Cabinet Office (1987) *Understanding Stress, Part One: A Line Manager's Guide*, London, HMSO.

Cade, B. (1983) 'Snuffed Out Fire Within', *Social Work Today*, 11 January 1983.

Caplan, G. (1961) *A Community Approach to Mental Health*, London, Tavistock.

Caplan, G. (1967) 'The Family as a Support System', in Caplan and Killea (1967).

Caplan, G. and Killea, M. (eds) (1967) *Support Systems and Mutual Help*, New York, Grune & Stratton.

Carkhuff, R. R. and Berenson, B. C (1977) *Beyond Counselling and Therapy*, 2nd edn, New York, Holt, Rinehart & Winston.

CCETSW (1991) *One Small Step Towards Racial Justice*, London, CCETSW.

CD Project Steering Group (eds) (1991) *Setting the Context for Change*, London, CCETSW.

Centre for Occupational Studies (1991) 'Code of Practice for Staff Care in the Health and Social Services', Keele, University of Keele/LGTB.

Cherniss, C. (1980) *Staff Burnout: Job Stress in the Human Services*, London, Sage.

Cherniss, C., Egnatios, E., Wacker, S. and O'Dowd, W. (1979) 'The Professional Mystique and Burnout in Public Sector Professionals', unpublished paper, University of Michigan, Ann Arbor.

Clarke, J. (1988) *Social Work: The Personal and the Political*, Open University, Unit 13 of D211, Social Problems and Social Welfare.

Clarke, M. and Stewart, J. (1988) *Managing Tomorrow*, Luton, LGTB.

Cohen, S. and Willis, T. A. (1985) 'Stress, Social Support and the Buffering Hypothesis', *Psychological Bulletin*, 98.

Coleman, V. (1988) *Stress Management Techniques*, London, Mercury Business Paperbacks.

Cooper, C. L. and Davidson, M. (1982) *High Pressure: Working Lives of Women Managers*, London, Fontana.

Cooper, C. L. and Makin, P. (eds) (1984) *Psychology for Managers*, London, Macmillan.

Cooper, C. L. and Marshall, J. (1976) 'Occupational Sources of Stress: A Review of the Literature Relating to Coronary Heart Disease and Mental Health', *Journal of Occupational Psychology*, 49.

Cooper, C. L. and Payne, R. (1980) *Current Concerns in Occupational Stress*, London, Wiley.

Cooper, C. L. and Payne, R. (eds) (1988) *Causes, Coping and Consequences of Stress at Work*, London, Wiley.

Cooper, C. L., Cooper, R. D. and Baker, L. (eds) (1988) *Living with Stress*, Harmondsworth, Penguin.

Corby, B. (1989) *Working with Child Abuse*, Buckingham, OpenUniversity Press.

Cousins, J. (1991) 'Take Charge', *Social Work Today*, 31 October 1991.

Coulshed, V. (1990) *Management in Social Work*, London, Macmillan.

Cox, T. (1987) 'Stress, Coping and Problem-solving', *Work and Stress*, 1 (1).

Crouter, A. C. (1984) 'Spill Over from Family to Work: The Neglected Side of the Work-Family Interface', *Human Relations*, 37.

Dale, P., Davies, M., Morrison, T. and Waters, J. (1986) *Dangerous Families*, London, Routledge.

Davison, G. C. and Neale, J. H. (1986) *Abnormal Psychology*, New York, Wiley.

DOH (Department of Health) (1991a) *Child Abuse: A Study of Inquiry Reports 1980-1989*, London, HMSO.

DOH (Department of Health) (1991b) *The Children Act 1989 Guidance and Regulations, Volume 4: Residential Care*, London, HMSO.

DOH (Department of Health) (1991c) *Working Together under the Children Act 1989*, London, HMSO.

Dominelli, L. (1989) 'An Uncaring Profession? An Examination of Racism in Social Work', *New Community*, 15(3).

Dunham, J. (1988) 'Review of the Stress Research Literature in Three Helping Occupations', in McDerment (1988).

Edelwich, J. and Brodsky, A. (1980) *Burn-out: Stages of Disillusionment in the Helping Professions*, New York, Human Sciences Press.

Etzioni, E. (ed.) (1969) *The Semi-Professions and their Organisation*, New York, Free Press.

Ferns, P. (1987) 'The Dangerous Delusion', *Community Care*, 8 January 1987.

Fielder, F. E. (1967) *A Theory of Leadership Effectiveness*, New York, McGraw-Hill.

Fineman, S. (1985) *Social Work Stress and Intervention*, Aldershot, Gower.

Fogarty, M. (1987) 'Women Social Workers Talking...', *Social Work Today*, 26 October 1987.

Folkman, S. (1984) 'Personal Control and Stress and Coping Processes: A Theoretical Analysis', *Journal of Personality and Social Psychology*, 46.

Folkman, S. and Lazarus, R. S. (1980) 'An Analysis of Coping in a Middle-Aged Community Sample', *Journal of Health and Social Behaviour*, 21.

Folkman, S., Lazarus, R. S., Dunkel-Schetter, C., Delongis, A. and Gruen, R. J. (1986) 'Dynamics of a Stressful Encounter: Cognitive Appraisal, Coping, and Encounter Outcomes', *Journal of Personality and Social Psychology*, 50.

Frankl, V. E. (1973) *Psychotherapy and Existentialism*, Harmondsworth, Penguin.

Freud, S. (1933) *New Introductory Lectures on Psychoanalysis*, Standard Edition 22, London, Hogarth Press.

Freudenberger, H. (1975) 'Staff Burnout', *Journal of Social Issues*, 30 (1).

Gale, H. de (1991) 'Black Students' Views of Existing CQSW Courses and CSS Schemes: 2', in CD Project Steering Group (1991).

George, L. K. (1989) 'Stress, Social Support and Depression over the Life-Course', in Markides and Cooper (1989).

Gibson, F., McGrath, A. and Reid, N. (1989) 'Occupational Stress in Social Work', *British Journal of Social Work*, 19.

Girdano, D. A., Everly, G. S. and Dusk, D. (1990) *Controlling Stress and Tension*, New York, Prentice-Hall.

Goldstein, H. (1973) *Social Work Practice; A Unitary Approach*, Carolina, University of South Carolina Press.

Gore, S. (1978) 'The Effect of Social Support in Moderating the Health Consequences of Unemployment', *Journal of Health and Social Behaviour*, 19.

Guteck, B., Repetti, R. and Silver, D. (1988) 'Non-Work Roles and Stress at Work', in Cooper and Payne (1988).

Hackman, J. K. and Oldham, G. R. (1980) *Work Design*, Reading, Mass., Addison-Wesley.

Hall, S. (1980) 'Race, Articulation and Societies Structured in Dominance', in UNESCO (1980).

Handy, C. (1985) *Understanding Organisations*, Harmondsworth, Penguin.

Hanmer, J. and Statham, D. (1988) *Women and Social Work*, London, Macmillan.

Harper, J. and Murphy, M. (1993) 'Child Protection Work: A Case for Multi-Disciplinary Staff Care', unpublished paper.

Haynes, S. and Feinleib, M. (1982) 'Women Work and Coronary Heart Disease: Prospective Findings from the Framingham Heart Study', *American Journal of Public Health*, 70.

Heather, N. (1976) *Radical Perspectives in Psychology*, London, Methuen.

Hemsley, J. (1986) 'Slow to Come Forward', *Community Care*, 5 June 1986.

Hickson, D. J., Butler, R. J., Cray, D., Mallory, G. R., and Wilson, D. C. (1986) *Top Decisions: Strategic Decision-Making in Organisations*, Oxford, Basil Blackwell.

Hobfall, S. E. (1988) *The Ecology of Stress*, New York, Hemisphere.

Holmes, T. H. and Rahe, R. H. (1967) 'The Social Readjustment Rating Scale', *Journal of Psychosomatic Research*, II.

Hopkins, J. (1987a) 'Meeting the Care Needs of Staff in the PSS', *Social Work Today*, 16 November 1987.

Hopkins, J. (1987b) 'The Sexual Harassment of Social Workers', *Social Work Today*, 26 October 1987.

Hopson, B. (1984), 'Transition: Understanding and Managing Personal Change', in Cooper and Makin (1984).

House, J. S. (1981) *Social Support and Stress*, Reading, Mass., Addison-Wesley.

Howe D. (1986a) *Social Workers and their Practice in Welfare Bureaucracies*, Aldershot, Gower.

Howe, D. (1986b) 'The Segregation of Women and Their Task in the Personal Social Services', *Critical Social Policy*, 15.

Hugman, R. (1991) *Power in Caring Professions*, London, Macmillan.

Hutchinson-Reis, M. (1989) '"And for Those of Us who are Black?" Black Politics in Social Work', in Langan and Lee (1989).

John, G. (1991)', "Taking Sides" Objectives and Strategies in the Development of Anti-Racist Work in Britain', in CD Project Steering Group (1991).

Johnstone, J. H. and Sarason, I. G. (1978) 'Lifestress, Depression and Anxiety: Internal-External Locus of Control as a Moderator Variable', *Journal of Psychosomatic Research*, 22.

Jones, F., Fletcher, B. C. and Ibbetson, K. (1991) 'Stressors and Strains amongst Social Workers: Demands, Supports, Constraints and Psychological Health', *British Journal of Social Work*, 21.

Judd, D. (1992) 'Psychic Trauma in Response to Life-threatening Illness', paper presented at the Second International Conference on Children and Death, Edinburgh.

Kadushin, A. (1974) *Child Welfare Services*, New York, Macmillan.

Kahn, R. L., Wolfe, D. M., Quinn, R. P., Snoek, J. D. and Rosenthal, R. A. (1964) *Organisational Stress: Studies in Role Conflict and Ambiguity*, New York, Wiley.

Kanter, R. M. (1983) *The Change Masters*, London, Unwin.

Kearns, J. (1986) *Stress at Work: The Challenge of Change*, London, BUPA.

Kendall, P. C. (ed.) (1986) *Advances in Cognitive-Behavioral Research and Therapy: Vol. 5*, New York, Academic Press.

Kirschner, D. A. and Kirschner, S. (1986) *Comprehensive Family Therapy: An Integration of Systematic and Psychodynamic Models*, New York, Bruner.

Kline, P. (1972) *Fact and Fiction in Freudian Theory*, London, Methuen.

Kobasa, S. C. (1979) 'Stressful Life Events, Personality, Health: An Enquiry into Hardiness', *Journal of Personality and Social Psychology*, 37.

Kobasa, S. C., Maddi, S. R. and Kahn, S. (1982) 'Hardiness and Health: A Prospective Study' *Journal of Personality and Social Psychology*, 42.

Kobasa, S. C. and Puccetti, M. C. (1983) 'Personality and Social Resources in Stress Resistance', *Journal of Personality and Social Psychology*, 45.

Laing, R. D. (1971) *The Politics of the Family*, Harmondsworth, Penguin.

Langan, M. (1992) 'Introduction', in Langan and Day (1992).

Langan, M. and Day, L. (eds) (1992) *Women, Oppression and Social Work*, London, Routledge.

Langan, M. and Lee, P. (eds) (1989) *Radical Social Work Today*, London, Unwin Hyman.

Lawrence, M. (1992) 'Women's Psychology and Feminist Social Work Practice', in Langan and Day (1992).

Lazarus, R. S. (1966) *Psychological Stress and the Coping Process*, New York, McGraw-Hill.

Lazarus, R. S. and Folkman, S. (1986) *Stress, Appraisal and Coping*, New York, Springer.

Levy, P. and Kahan, B. (1991) *The Pindown Experience*, Staffordshire County Council.

LGTB (1988) *Going for Better Management*, London, Local Government Training Board.

Looker, T. and Gregson, O. (1989) *Stresswise*, Sevenoaks, Hodder & Stoughton.

Lupton, C. (1992) 'Feminism, Managerialism and Performance Measurement', in Langan and Day (1992).

Maddi, S. R. and Kobasa, S. C. (1984) *The Hardy Executive: Health under Stress*, Homewood Ill., Dow Jones Irwin.

Markides, K. and Cooper, C. L. (eds) (1989) *Aging, Stress and Health*, New York, Wiley.

Martin, R. A. and Lefcourt, H. M. (1983) 'Sense of Humour as a Moderator of the Relation Between Stressors and Moods', *Journal of Personality and Social Psychology*, 45.

Maslach, C. and Jackson, S. (1981) *The Maslach Burnout Inventory*, Palo Alto, Cal., Consulting Psychology Press.

Maslach, C. and Jackson, S. (1982) 'Burnout in Health Professionals: A Social Psychological Analysis', in Sanders and Juls (1982).

Masson, H. and Morrison, T. (1991) 'A 24 Hour Duty System: Using Practitioner Research to Manage the Stress', *British Journal of Social Work*, 21.

Mathews, K. A. and Haynes, S. G. (1986) 'Type A Behaviour Pattern and Coronary Disease Risk: Update and Critical Evaluation', *American Journal of Epidemiology*, 123.

McDerment, L. (ed.) (1988) *Stress Care*, Surbiton, Social Care Association.

McDerment, L. (1992) 'Present Tense, Future Perfect', *Care Weekly*, 13 August 1992.

McGee, R. A. (1989) 'Burnout and Professional Decision-Making', *Journal of Counselling Psychology*, July, 1989.

Megranahan, M. (1983) *Counselling: A Practical Guide for Employers*, London, IPM.

Meichenbaum, D. (1985) *Stress Inoculation Training*, Oxford, Pergamon.

Melhuish, A. (1978) *Executive Stress*, London, Business Books.

Mills, A. J. and Murgatroyd, S. J. (1991) *Organizational Rules*, Buckingham, Open University Press.

Mintzberg, H. (1988) 'Crafting Strategy', *McKinsey Quarterly Seminar*, Summer, 1988.

Morgan, G. (1986) *Images of Organization*, California, Sage.

Morrison, T. (1990) 'The Emotional Effects of Child Protection Work on the Worker', *Practice*, 4 (4).

Morrison, T. (1993) *Supervision in Social Care: An Action Learning Approach*, London, Longman.

Morrison, T., Waters, J., Roberts, W., Craig E., Steane, E. and Erooga, M. (1987) *Surviving in Teams*, Rochdale Child Protection Training Sub-Committee.

Murphy, M. (1991) 'Pressure Points', *Social Work Today*, 13 June 1991.

NALGO (1989) 'Social Work in Crisis', London, National and Local Government Officers' Association.

New, C. and David, M. (1985) *For the Children's Sake: Making Child Care More than Women's Business*, Harmondsworth, Penguin.

Newman, J. E. and Beehr, T. A. (1979) 'Personal and Organisational Strategies for Handling Job Stress: A Review of Research and Opinion', *Personnel Psychology*, 32.

Newton, T. and Keenan, A. (1985) 'Coping with Work-related Stress', *Human Relations*, 38(2).

Paine, W. (ed.), (1982) *Job Stress and Burnout*, London, Sage.

Payne, M. (1991) *Modern Social Work Theory: A Critical Introduction*, London, Macmillan.

Payne, R. (1980) 'Organisational Stress and Support', in Cooper and Payne (1980).

Peck, D. and Whitlow, D. (1975) *Approaches To Personality Theory*, London, Methuen.

Phillipson, J. (1992) *Practising Equality: Women, Men and Social Work*, London, CCETSW.

Pincus, G. (ed.) (1959) *Hormones and Atherosclerosis*, New York, Academic Press.

Pines, A. and Kafry, D. (1978) 'Occupational Tedium in the Social Services', *National Association of Social Workers*, November 1978.

Pink, D. (1991) 'Black Students' Views of Existing CQSW Courses and CSS Schemes: 1', in CD Project Steering Group (1991).

Pottage, D. and Evans, M. (1992) *Workbased Stress: Prescription is Not the Cure*, London, NISW.

Preston-Shoot, M. and Braye, S. (1991) 'Managing the Personal Experience of Work', *Practice*, 5(1).

Pynoos, R. and Eth, S. (1984) 'The Child as Witness to Homicide', *Journal of Social Issues*, 40(2).

Quick, J. C. and Quick, J. D. (1984) *Organisational Stress and Preventative Management*, New York, McGraw Hill.

Ramdin, R. (1987) *The Making of the Black Working Class in Britain*, Aldershot, Gower.

Randell, G., Packard, P. and Slater, J. (1984) *Staff Appraisal*, London, IPM.

Raphael, B. (1990) *When Disaster Strikes*, 2nd edn, London, Unwin Hyman.

Rees, S. and Graham, R. S. (1991) *Assertion Training*, London, Routledge.

Richards, M. and Payne, C., with Sheppard, A. (1990) *Staff Supervision in Child Protection*, London, NISW.

Rickford, F. (1992) 'Monster of a Job', *Social Work Today*, 30 January 1992.

Rojek, C., Peacock, G. and Collins, S. (1988) *Social Work and Received Ideas*, London, Routledge.

Rosenman, R. H. and Friedman, N. I. (1959) 'The Possible Relationship of the Emotions to Coronary Heart Disease', in Pincus (1959).

Rosenman, R. H., Friedman, N. I. and Strauss, R. (1966) 'Coronary Heart Disease in the Western Collaborative Group Study', *Journal of American Medical Association*, 195.

Rotter, J. B. (1954) *Social Learning and Clinical Psychology*, Englewood Cliffs, N.J., Prentice-Hall.

Rotter, J. B. (1966) 'Generalised Expectancies for Internal versus External Control of Reinforcement', *Psychological Monographs* 30(1).

Rotter, J. B. and Hochreich, D. J. (1975) *Personality*, Glenview, Ill., Scott, Foresman.

Rychman, R. M. (1978) *Theories of Personality*, New York, Van Nostrand.

Salaman, G. (ed.) (1992) *Human Resource Strategies*, London, Sage.

Sancler, I. N. and Lakey, E. (1982) 'Locus of Control as a Stress Moderator: The Role of Control, Perceptions and Social Support', *American Journal of Community Psychology*, 10.

Sanders, G. and Juls, J. (eds) (1982) *The Social Psychology of Health and Illness*, Hillside, N.J., Erlbaum.

Satir, V. (1975) *Self Esteem*, Milbrae, Cal., Celestial Arts.

Satyamurti, C. (1981) *Occupational Survival*, Oxford, Pergamon.

Schulz, R. and Decker, S. (1985) 'Long Term Adjustment to Physical Disability: The Role of Social Support, Perceived Control and Self Blame', *Journal of Personality and Social Psychology*, 48.

Schwartz, R. M. and Garamoni, G. L. (1986) 'A Structural Model of Positive and Negative States of Mind: Asymmetry in the Internal Dialogue', in Kendall (1986).

Scott, M. J. and Stradling, S. G. (1992) *Counselling for Post-Traumatic Stress Disorder*, London, Sage.

Scott, M. J. and Stradling, S. G. (1993) 'Post-traumatic Stress Without the Trauma', *British Journal of Clinical Psychology*, 32(3).

Seligman, M. E. P. (1975) *Helplessness*, San Francisco, Freeman.

Selye, H. (1974) *Stress Without Distress*, Sevenoaks, Hodder & Stoughton.

Skinner, B. F. (1974) *About Behaviourism*, New York, Knopf.

Smith, M. (1992) 'Utility and Human Resource Management', Unit 13, Supplementary Readings for the Open University Course: B884 Human Resource Strategies.

Smith, M., Beck, J., Cooper, C. L., Cox, C., Ottoway, D. and Talbot, R. (1982) *Introducing Organisational Behaviour*, London, Macmillan.

SSI (Social Services Inspectorate) (1991) *Women in Social Services: A Neglected Resource*, London, HMSO.

Souza, P. de (1991) 'A Review of the Experiences of Black Students in Social Work Training', in CCETSW (1991).

Spielberger, C. (1979) *Understanding Stress and Anxiety*, London, Harper & Row.

Spielberger, C. and Sarason, I. G. (eds) (1978) *Stress and Anxiety*, Vol. 5, New York, Hemisphere.

Stevenson, O. (1991) 'Social Work Intervention: Aspects of Research and Practice', paper presented at the BASPCAN Conference, Leicester.

Stevenson, O. and Parsloe P. (1978) *Social Services Teams: The Practitioner's View*, London, HMSO.

Stone, M. (1990) *Child Protection Work: A Professional Guide*, Birmingham, Venture Press.

Storey, J. (1992) 'Human Resource Management in the Public Sector', in Salaman (1992).

Sutherland, V. and Cooper, C. L. (1991) *Understanding Stress: A Perspective for Health Professionals*, London, Chapman & Hall.

Tache, J. and Selye, H. (1978) 'On Stress and Coping Mechanisms', in Spielberger and Sarason (1978).

Taylor, S. (1983) 'Adjustment to Life Events: A Theory of Cognitive Adaptation', *American Psychologist*, 38.

Taylor, S. and Brown, J. D. (1980) 'Illusion and Well-being: A Social Psychological Perspective on Mental Health', *Psychological Bulletin*, 103.

Thompson, N. (1990) 'The Uncertainty Principle in Teaching Social Work and Social Science', *Social Science Teacher*, 19 (2).

Thompson, N. (1991a) 'Breaking Cycles', *Community Care*, 31 January 1991.

Thompson, N. (1991b) *Crisis Intervention Revisited*, Birmingham, Pepar.

Thompson, N. (1991c) 'The Legacy of Laing: A Critique of the Medical Model in Social Work and Social Care', *Social Science Teacher*, 20 (2).

Thompson, N. (1992a) *Existentialism and Social Work*, Aldershot, Avebury.

Thompson, N. (1992b) *Child Abuse: the Existential Dimension*, University of East Anglia Social Work Monographs.

Thompson, N. (1993) *Anti-Discriminatory Practice*, London, Macmillan.

Thompson, N., Osada, M. and Anderson, B. (1990) *Practice Teaching in Social Work: A Handbook*, Birmingham, Pepar.

Thompson, S. C. (1981) 'Will It Hurt Less If I Can Control It? A Complex Answer to a Simple Question', *Psychological Bulletin*, 90.

Toffler, A. (1970) *Future Shock*, London, Bodley Head.

Torrington, D. and Hall. L. (1988), *Personnel Management*, New York, Prentice Hall.

Torrington, D., Weightman, J. and Johns, K. (1985) *Management Methods*, London, IPM.

Totman, R. (1990) *Mind, Stress and Health*, London, Souvenir Press.

Tubesing, N. L. and Tubesing, D. A (1982) 'The Treatment of Choice: Selecting Stress Skills to Suit the Individual and the Situation', in Paine (1982).

UNESCO (1980) *Sociological Theories: Race and Colonialism*, Paris, UNESCO.

Wade, C. (1970) *Natural Ways To Health Through Controlled Fasting*, New York, Arch Books.

Wade, C. and Tavris, C. (1990) *Psychology*, London, Harper & Row.

Walsh, J. A. (1987) 'Burnout and Values in the Social Service Profession', *The Journal of Contemporary Social Work*, May 1987.

Warr, P. and Payne, R. (1982) 'Experiences of Strain and Pleasure among British Adults', *Social Science and Medicine*, 16.

Webb, A. (1989) 'Organisational Responses to Occupational Stress and Stressful Incidents in Residential Child Care, unpublished dissertation, University of Manchester.

Webb, R. and Tossell, D. (1991) *Social Issues for Carers*, London, Edward Arnold.

Weinstein, H. M. and Zappert, L. T. (1985) 'Sex Differences in the Impact of Work on Physical and Psychological Health', *American Journal of Psychiatry*, October (1985).

Weintraub, J. K., Carver, C. and Scheier, M. (1989) 'Assessing Coping Strategies: A Theoretically-based Approach', *Journal of Personality and Social Psychology*, 56 (2).

Wiener, R. (1989) 'Stress Within the Team', *Social Work Today*, 11 May 1989.

Wilkinson, R. and Wilson, G. (1992) 'Pressure Points', *Social Work Today*, 11 June 1992.

Williams, F. (1989) *Social Policy: A Critical Introduction*, London, Polity.

Index